A Journey through Grief and Healing with the Holy Spirit

WONDERFUL

Counselor

Alicia Crawley

CROSSBOOKS
PUBLISHING

CrossBooks™
A Division of LifeWay
1663 Liberty Drive
Bloomington, IN 47403
www.crossbooks.com
Phone: 1-866-879-0502

All Scripture quotes are from NLT 1996 unless otherwise noted

Other versions used and noted in text: Message, NIV, KJV, AMP, CEV, NJB, NKJV

First published by CrossBooks 11/15/2011

ISBN: 978-1-4627-0678-5 (sc)
ISBN: 978-1-4627-1122-2 (e)

Library of Congress Control Number: 2011918280

Printed in the United States of America

This book is printed on acid-free paper.

For Christ Jesus my King.
May you be forever worshiped
for your power
to save and heal the broken.

And for Lauren Michelle,
my beautiful daughter
with whom I cannot wait to spend eternity
in the presence of our King.

"And we have received God's Spirit (not the world's spirit), so we can know the wonderful things God has freely given us."

1 Corinthians 2:12

Contents

Preface

If you are old enough to read this sentence, you've probably discovered that the world is not all it promises to be. Our childlike wonder and idealistic desire to fulfill our dreams are eventually tempered by reality. Broken relationships, bad decisions, disappointments, tragedy and loss come to us all in one form or another. Of course there are real joys in life as well, and some dreams do come true. We do well to embrace these good gifts from God with gratitude and contentment.

But trials inevitably come, for this world is broken by sin. All of us go our own way, pursuing self instead of God. And oh, how wise He is to allow the very consequences of our sin to break us and turn us to Him. He can only do this, though, when we are humble enough to see our broken ways, and broken*ness*.

It seems to me, as I look around, that we're becoming pretty good at recognizing brokenness in our lives. (We've always been able to recognize it in others!) Some choose to ignore it, stuffing it deep inside, and some try to cover it up by any number of means—distractions, busyness, achievement or addictions. But others reach out for help. The question is, *where do we turn when we experience things that break us and we realize we need help?* The world turns to any number of options: self-help books and seminars, support groups, therapists, psychology, and medication. All of these avenues can be very helpful and good choices. Today, many Christians receive the help they need from these sources, especially if they find God-centered ones.

My purpose in this book is not to discount any of the ways to get help listed above. I believe God gave us the ability to pursue knowledge and understanding in order to have healthier lives. I'm thankful for medical and psychological breakthroughs that have shed light on my problems and those of our society and world. I've read any number of books and articles in search of help with my own hurts and brokenness.

Rather than tossing those things out, I want instead to explore with you what I believe to be a tragically ignored resource available to every follower of Christ. It is by far the greatest we could ever hope to find, one that far exceeds any human effort. What is this resource? I'm talking about the Holy Spirit, who lives in everyone who has put their trust in the Lord Jesus Christ. This third member of the Trinity has been so misunderstood, misrepresented, and even feared, that we no longer realize the amazing gift He truly is.

Jesus said in John 14, *"And I will ask the Father, and he will give you another Counselor, who will never leave you. He is the Holy Spirit, who leads into all truth"* (v. 16). Later, He remarked, *"But it is actually best for you that I go away, because if I don't, the Counselor won't come. If I do go away, he will come because I will send him to you"* (John 16:7). The Holy Spirit Jesus promised now lives inside of every believer. He is called many things—Comforter, Encourager, Advocate, Counselor. What an incredible gift! Jesus valued the Holy Spirit so much that He saw leaving His disciples as a good thing, because it was the only way He could send the Spirit to them.

Why was it better for them to have the Holy Spirit *in* them rather than the physical Jesus *with* them? Because the Holy Spirit could actually transform them from the inside out. And He could be their power source for all He wanted to accomplish through them. It's easy to see the difference the Holy Spirit made in the disciples' own lives. After the resurrection, they had the *risen* Christ with them, yet they still hid behind closed doors, didn't know their purpose (why did they return to their fishing business in Galilee?), and thought Jesus' next move would be to establish His earthly kingdom (see Acts 1:6). But after Jesus ascended, the Holy Spirit came to them on the day of Pentecost. They became an unstoppable force such as the world had ever seen. Three thousand people turned to Christ that day, and soon after, 5000 more were added. The disciples then took the Gospel to the Gentile world, and almost all of them were eventually martyred for their faith and boldness.

The difference? The Holy Spirit *in* them.

But how does this relate to our lives today? Believers are still called to take the Gospel to the world and this can only be done through the power of the Holy Spirit living in us. But is this the only work of the Holy Spirit? No, for I believe there is life-giving, healing, and transforming work He does on the inside of each of us. This work is essential to the outward work of changing the world, because He does it one heart at a time. As we are healed and changed, He heals and changes the world around us, through us.

So where am I going with all this? Let's go back to my original premise, that in our world today, believers turn most often to human sources of help when they are hurting and broken. They largely ignore their greatest resource, the Holy Spirit, our Counselor. The following pages are my own journey of brokenness, loss, and healing, and how, by His grace, God led me to seek His counsel day after day. When it was all I could do to get out of bed, and the thought of facing another day threatened to overwhelm me, He drew me gently to meet with Him. During the process, I didn't recognize myself or my life anymore, much less what He was doing in me. But as I progressed, He showed me He was healing me one day at a time. His Word was life to me, His truth the healing balm that made me able to go on. Not only that, but the Holy Spirit's power worked through me. He gave me the strength to find joy again in the work of His Kingdom.

Along the way, I shared with close friends some of the things God was teaching me. Occasionally one of them would urge me to write a book, but I didn't seriously consider it. I eventually had at least ten journals recording my times with the Holy Spirit in His Word. But, I didn't want to publish them without a clear purpose or message. There were many grief books already available, and I didn't think I had anything significant to add.

One day in early fall of 2010, two-and-a-half years into my grief journey, I was again considering a question I asked myself many times: *Should I have sought professional counseling or joined a grief support group?* Throughout the process of grief, I never felt comfortable doing so. I couldn't pinpoint why, I just felt that it would not address my needs. But, when I asked the question that day, I heard the Holy

Spirit answer me: *I have been your counselor; you didn't need anything else.*

Thinking about it, I realized it was true. The Holy Spirit met every need, answered every question (in His way, not mine), and brought incredible healing to me in the Word of God every day. I *didn't* need anything else. He alone knew how to walk me through grief. He addressed its complicated issues in the right order for my unique way of processing it all. If I had reached an impasse or found myself unable to connect with God, I would have sought Bible-based professional help. I encourage anyone to do so if they need it.

But God had a different grief journey in mind for me, for a reason. That fall day in 2010, God gave me the message I was to share in a book based on my journals. It was a message I hadn't read in any other book: The Holy Spirit is my *Wonderful Counselor*, the greatest resource I have as a child of God. He carried me better than anyone could have through the darkest valley of my life, bringing me to healing on the other side.

I've been asked what is the one grief book that helped me most. For a long time, this was hard to answer. I would eventually come up with a book or two, always based on Scripture. That question, and compiling this book from my journals, made me realize that the best grief book is the Bible, hands down. It's also the best marriage book, parenting book, financial advice book, and life-management book. In fact, the Bible is the best book on any topic a person might need to seek help for. *But it must be read with the help of the Holy Spirit.* The best Counselor using the best book of Counsel brings the most wisdom and healing to anyone in any situation.

The following pages share three years of intense grief counseling I received from the Holy Spirit of Jesus Christ. They are filled with scripture, narration, and journal entries, and divided into topics. The story is fairly chronological, but also takes each topic individually from start to finish. By revealing how God met me in the depths of my pain, it's my prayer that you'll see how completely God's Word addresses the hardest questions, and how the Holy Spirit beautifully applies its wisdom to our greatest needs.

I haven't come to the place of total healing, for that will only happen when I stand before Jesus face to face. But I have come to a place of greater healing, wholeness and fulfillment than I have ever known. And because the Holy Spirit walked me through the process, He was able to deepen my relationship with Christ beyond anything I could have ever dreamed. I know Him better than I ever have. I believe that was part of His purpose in my journey all along. I want to continue this journey from brokenness to wholeness with Him, my *Wonderful Counselor*. And I want you to do the same. Most importantly, *He* wants you to do it, to take your own journey with Him to wholeness and intimate relationship with Him.

My prayer for you is this:

> *"Keep on asking, and you will be given what you ask for. Keep on looking, and you will find. Keep on knocking, and the door will be opened. For everyone who asks, receives. Everyone who seeks, finds. And the door is opened to everyone who knocks...how much more will your heavenly Father give the Holy Spirit to those who ask him?"*

Luke 11:9-10, 13

Acknowledgements

No book is written alone. First and foremost, I must thank the Holy Spirit of Jesus Christ. You are the one who lovingly wrote this message one day at a time in my heart and in my journals. It is Your wisdom, Your truth, Your story. It would not have been written without You. I am forever Yours.

To my husband, Scott, thank you for your unwavering love for me, and for your enthusiastic support of this book. You have cheered me on, sharing priceless insights on the nature of God with me. You walked with me day after day through our grief, as we cried and prayed together. You allow me to leave you with the kids as I answer God's call to go in His name, and you let me worship beside you. You are the love of my life, second only to our first love, the Lord Jesus Christ.

To my boys, Jordan and Jonathan. You are the most amazing young men I know and I am so proud of you. Lauren loved you deeply while she was here, and I know she eagerly anticipates the day she will see you again. So do I. For now, I am deeply grateful to God for each day He gifts me with your presence in this world. I know you will follow Jesus all the days of your life. I love you both with all my heart.

I want to thank the people who made this book possible by sharing their valuable talents with me. To my friend, Dana Drummond, for your expert editing and advice, and for your personal encouragement. Dana, I cannot put a price tag on your help and support. This book would not be what it is without you.

Thanks also to many of my friends and family who proof-read chapters for me: my mom, Patty Houser; my sister, Vicki Schmidt; my mother-in-law, Dixie Crawley; my sister-in-law, Tammy Crawley; Leah Horner; Jamie Watkins; Rebecca Brown; Andrea Graver; Wendy English; Alisa Wilburn; Tammy Vincent; and Courtney Bullard. I appreciate so much your willingness to help and the objective eye you lent to this project. Far beyond that, your friendship means more to me than you will ever know. All of you played a big part in my healing as the hands and feet of Christ. I love you.

To my "safe people:" Judy, Alisa, Gwen, Julie, Andrea, Tammy, Wendy, Courtney, Melissa. Wow, I am blessed! Thank you for letting me not be okay. I can never repay you and I love you.

To the many others who walked with us through the valley and carried us with your prayers and practical gifts. I wish I could name you all, but there are too many to count.

To Kathy Sue Roberts, for the pictures she donated for this project: the beautiful headshot of Lauren, and the family photo. Thank you for sharing your talent with us and for loving our daughter.

To Brenda Horan, for the free gift of a photo shoot and author headshot. What a gift from a new friend in Christ! May God bless your ministry.

Chapter 1—Springs of Living Water

I entered the story of God in 1964, the first child of my parents, who provided a wonderful Christian home for me. I have a younger sister and brother, and all three of us were reared in a faith lived out before us. We all embraced this faith, a blessing to my parents because of their faithfulness to God.

Happily ever after, right? No. The human story never quite goes like that, and neither does mine. I share my beginnings to show: 1) I have no real family dysfunction I can blame for my own broken condition; and 2) the work of God in a life is completely supernatural. My parents will, I have no doubt, be richly rewarded in heaven for what they sowed into our lives. Even now, God has produced much fruit in our family because of their faithfulness. But their efforts to lead me to embrace faith in Christ couldn't guarantee that I would do so.

Ultimately, I could only experience new life in Christ through the work of the Holy Spirit in my heart. And while the seeds of faith were sown into my life in childhood, that true saving work came years after I left home and began a family of my own. Until then, I lived under a faulty understanding of God. I saw Him as a loving God, but more in a dutiful, general sense than as a God of personal love. He might love the world, but surely His "love" for me could only be out of obligation. I was such a mess inside that I thought He could barely tolerate me and was always disappointed in my failed efforts to be a godly person. I could do many outwardly good things: direct children's activities at church, sing in the choir, read my Bible and teach it to my children. But even these things were an effort, and I often fell into bad behavior—fits of anger, complaining, and judging others. I hated not being able to change myself, and I walked under a cloud of guilt over failing constantly. Out of that cloud, I envisioned God's disappointed gaze falling on me.

In January of 2001, God began a new work in my heart. My marriage of seventeen years was troubled, largely because of my attitude and actions toward my husband, Scott. Though he would never have left, Scott distanced himself from me over time as I became more controlling and dissatisfied. We would have stayed together no matter how estranged my behavior made us. But God had something better in mind.

Shortly after Christmas, I read *The Prayer of Jabez* by Bruce Wilkinson. I prayed, "Lord, bless me indeed!" from that prayer, not knowing what in the world I was praying for. But God knew. He poured out the blessing of softening my heart toward my husband. I stopped nagging and putting demands on Scott to satisfy my cavernous need for love and affirmation. I no longer tried to control him, "freeing" him to be himself without angry repercussions from me. Scott immediately recognized the difference in me and still mentions it occasionally today. I can only explain this change in me as a work of the Holy Spirit preparing my heart for what He was about to do next.

In early April, 2001, several events transpired that opened my eyes to the true nature of God's passionate and personal love for me. The first was an Easter production at my sister Vicki's church. My six-year-old nephew Brian played a crippled child healed by Jesus. As "Jesus" held and loved this boy that I loved, God spoke to my heart. "My love is real and personal, not distant and dutiful. I am in love with this one you know. *I am in love with you.*"

Days later, I read *He Chose the Nails,* by Max Lucado, in which he explores all that Christ suffered for our salvation: Why did He choose the nails? The crown of thorns? The whip? The spear? Why did He give up His robe? His life?

"I did it just for you." (p.9)

For me? Just for me? Could He really love me that much?

In *He Chose the Nails,* Lucado tells the story of a girl named Madeline and her father Joe. When Madeline was young, she and Joe would dance together every Christmas Eve. But as the years went by, Madeline sought a life without her father. Soon she was looking elsewhere for love, and refused to dance with Joe anymore. Eventually, she ran off with her boyfriend. When he deserted her, she ended up in a life she never dreamed of, a nightmare of doing things she was ashamed of just to survive. Once, an old acquaintance brought Madeline a box full of letters from her father that had come to his address. She was too ashamed to open any of them, sure that her father would hate her if he knew what she had become. But she kept them at the club where she worked, organized according to postmark. One night, she found a letter hand-delivered to her at work. She opened it and read, "I know where you are. I know what you do. This doesn't change the way I feel. What I've said in each letter is still true."

"But I don't know what you've said," Madeline declared. She pulled a letter from the top of the stack in the box and read it. Then she read a second and a third. Each letter had the same sentence. Each sentence asked the same question.

Madeline raced to her father's home, hoping to make it in time. When she came in the door on Christmas Eve, someone went to find Joe. He came to meet her and she said,

"The answer is 'yes.' If the invitation is still good, the answer is 'yes.'"

Joe swallowed hard. "Oh my. The invitation is good."

And so the two danced again on Christmas Eve.

On the floor, near the door, rested a letter with Madeline's name and her father's request.

"Will you come home and dance with your poppa again?" (p. 68)[1]

As I read this story of a father's love for his daughter, my eyes opened wide to the truth of God's pursuing love *for me*. Could God really love me that way, just the way I was? Was He actually pursuing me with passion and desire? It seemed too good to be true. This God I had tried to love for so long, yet only feared and resented, loved me!

A huge weight of guilt and shame lifted from my heart that day. I had not disappointed Him by failing to become someone He could love. He loved me already. And only that

---

[1]   Max Lucado, *He Chose the Nails* (Nashville: Thomas Nelson, 2000), adapted and excerpted from 59-68.

love would set me free to become everything I wanted to be for Him, but could never be on my own.

In the days that followed, I came to understand the true nature of God's heart toward me. It is a heart of tender and passionate desire for relationship with me as His beloved child. Suddenly the floodgates opened wide and I was swept away in a torrent of mercy, love and grace. It brought me literally to my knees before this One who had poured Himself out for me on the cross. In joyful repentance, I surrendered my life to Jesus in complete abandon. Inside, I felt what I can only describe as a spring of water bursting through me, bringing me to life in a way I had never experienced. It was only later I realized that this is the very description Jesus gave of the Holy Spirit as He gives new life to someone: *"The water I give them takes away thirst altogether. It becomes a perpetual spring within them, giving them eternal life"* (John 4:14).

The Amplified Bible expands on this, saying, *"[It]shall become a spring of water welling up (flowing, bubbling) [continually] within him unto (into, for) eternal life."* Life now bubbled up inside of me. It was a quality of life different from anything I had ever known, and it flowed out from me in a response of love.

Jesus gave this invitation to all who would listen: *"If you are thirsty, come to me! If you believe in me, come and drink! For the Scriptures declare that rivers of living water will flow out from within"* (*John* 7:38). John then explains that the living water Jesus spoke of is the Holy Spirit. This is exactly what was happening inside of me. Centuries earlier, the Psalmist described the same thing:

> *"I hear the tumult of the raging seas*
> *as your waves and surging tides sweep over me.*

> *Through each day the LORD pours his unfailing*
> *love upon me,*
> *and through each night I sing his songs,*
> *praying to God who gives me life."*

Psalm 42:7-8

I know not everyone experiences the work of the Holy Spirit just like I did. Many have no initial sense of a change inside of them when they give their lives to Jesus Christ. But in testimony after testimony, people attest to the real and continual change the Holy Spirit works in their lives over time. They know they have been given new life. Why God chose to work the way He did in me, I can only speculate. I have a strong suspicion that it was because of my incredible hardness of head and heart. I spent thirty-seven years in the family of faith, surrounded by true believers. I was taught God's Word in every format imaginable. I saw example after example of the power of God's love to change a life. Yet I remained blind to His desire to do the same thing in me. Instead, my life was marked by a cold acceptance of the facts with no warming of my heart in trust of Christ's love for me. I must have needed a "Damascus Road"-type conversion to have one at all. And I believe time was running out for me to have it. But that is the subject of the next chapter.

At this point, God drew me into a more intimate time of getting to know Him, through His Word and Spirit, than I could ever have imagined. For the next several months, my schedule strangely open, I spent hours poring over God's Word. I soaked in its truths about His passionate and sacrificial love for His people. As I read, prayed, cried, and worshiped, I wondered how I could have missed it for so long. It was abundantly clear to me now in His Word, from Genesis to Revelation. I was like a parched, dead branch come alive, soaking in the water I hadn't even known I was thirsty for. Here are a few of the passages that spoke to my heart:

> *"Yet Jerusalem says, 'The Lord has deserted us; the Lord has forgotten us.' 'Never! Can a mother forget her nursing child? Can she feel no love for a child she has borne? But even if that were possible, I would not forget you! See, I have written your name on my hand.'"*

Isaiah 49:14-16

A picture of Jesus' crucifixion, my name carved by the nails into His hands.

> *"For the Lord your God has arrived to live among you. He is a mighty savior. He will rejoice over you with great gladness. With his love, he will calm all your fears. He will exult over you by singing a happy song."*

Zephaniah 3:17

What news it was to me that God loved me and sang over me because He was happy with me!

> *"Then Jesus said, 'Come to me, all of you who are weary and carry heavy burdens, and I will give you rest.'"*

Matthew 11:28

> *"And I am convinced that nothing can ever separate us from his love. Death can't and life can't. The angels can't and the demons can't. Our fears for*

7

today, our worries about tomorrow, and even the powers of hell can't keep God's love away. Whether we are high above the sky or in the deepest ocean, nothing in all creation will ever be able to separate us from the love of God that is revealed in Christ Jesus our Lord."

Romans 8:38-39

I also read scriptures that expressed my new-found love for Him:

"O God, you are my God;
I earnestly search for you.
my soul thirsts for you;
my whole body longs for you
in this parched and weary land
where there is no water.
I have seen you in your sanctuary
and gazed upon your power and glory.
Your unfailing love is better to me than life itself;
how I praise you!
I will honor you as long as I live,
lifting up my hands to you in prayer.
You satisfy me more than the richest of foods.
I will praise you with songs of joy."

Psalm 63:1-5

"I have been crucified with Christ. I myself no longer live, but Christ lives in me. So I live my life in this earthly body by trusting in the Son of God, who loved me and gave himself for me."

Galatians 2:20

That summer, my neighbor, Julie, introduced me to a discipleship study called *One on One with God* by Jerry and Marilyn Fine. Through it, I learned to nurture my budding relationship with Jesus by reading His Word, meditating on it, and responding in prayer to Him. I recorded these things, and my prayers of surrender to Him, in a journal. In just fifteen weeks, *One on One with God* gave me life-long tools to hear and respond to Jesus personally. In this way, I drew close to Him. I learned to listen to the Holy Spirit, recognizing His voice through His Word and in my spirit. My one-on-one relationship with Jesus grew, transforming me and sustaining me. I didn't know it then, but God was weaving into me the lifeline I would one day need to survive the fiercest of storms.

This new relationship with a God who loved me created huge changes in me; changes I had longed for and failed to achieve my entire life. Because the enormous hole inside my heart was finally being filled by the only One who *could* fill it, other things I had tried just fell away. Romance novels, soap operas, and talk shows disappeared from my life. So did the continual dissatisfaction with my husband's love that was stirred up by them. Not all of those things are bad; I just looked to them as idols. I tried to use them to replace what only God could give me. But being filled to overflowing with the love of God just washed away lesser things. My temper and my tendency to complain and criticize didn't control me anymore either. In no way was I perfected, not even close. Nor am I today. But I was alive! I was finally connected to the Source of all I was made for, never to be cut off again.

My relationships with others changed drastically during this time. As my need for unconditional love was met by Jesus Christ, I found myself free to love others unconditionally in the same way. I didn't try to love in order to be loved anymore, because I was *already* loved. I didn't have to demand love, because I was full of Christ's love for me. In fact, His love became the source of my love for others. I could love without expectations, satisfied in the love of Christ. But, as I rested in this love that still takes my breath away, a crazy thing happened. I received the love from my husband, children and friends that I had strived for so long.

My parenting changed too. Up to this time, I had reared Jordan, Lauren, and Jonathan to "behave," instead of trust and love God. It was the way I lived, so how could I teach them any differently? But when the love of Jesus changed me, it changed what I taught them too. Instead of focusing only on shaping my children's character and behavior, I began to try to reach their hearts with my amazing discovery: "God loves you! He made you to love you. Please understand how precious you are to Him." I couldn't keep it in. They had to know what I had finally learned, as early in their young lives as possible. I didn't want them to miss out on this amazing love relationship with Jesus for as long as I did. I knew that if they could understand and open their hearts to His love, God would do the rest. They would be transformed into His likeness by that love, not by anything I could do. I still trained them, as God commands parents to do, because that is an expression of His love (Hebrews 12:6-7). But He also placed urgency in my heart to pray continually that my sons and my daughter would not miss the love of Jesus Christ for them no matter what it took. At the time, I had no idea why this pressed on me so strongly.

But God did.

Our family, October 2007

Helicopter ride over Niagara Falls, Canada on a family
trip, Summer 2007

Jordan, Jonathan, and Lauren making faces.

More silly faces.

A kiss for Jonathan from his big sis.

Chapter 2—Plunged into the Valley

My new life in Christ began just as my oldest son, Jordan, was in middle school, a time of transition in so many ways. It can be scary for parents, and kids, who are growing up physically and socially. They seek connection outside the family, spending more time away from home, and they learn to think and believe for themselves. My prayers for all of my children became centered on wanting them to understand the great love of God for them personally. I knew that if their hearts received this truth, they would choose relationship with Him.

It wasn't easy to find the best ways to influence them toward Christ. I prayed with great concern for ideas to help them choose to personally embrace faith in Him. They had all made a "decision" to accept Christ as their Savior, but I knew if this was only a mental acceptance of the Gospel, it didn't guarantee they would trust His love for them. So, I asked God for ways to live the truth together with them and to help them see Him as He really is.

As the years went by, God's grace provided not only a home now filled with His love (and many redeemed mistakes too!), but also a church youth group that fostered their personal relationship with the God who loves them. My two older children, Jordan and Lauren, embraced that relationship. They, like me, were works in progress, often stumbling, but we walked the road together as God did His transforming work. Jordan excelled in music and found great joy in leading worship at school, church, and home. He would play worship music in his closet at night; Lauren would hear him through the wall and come to join him.

Lauren played basketball, but during the summer after her sophomore year in high school, she sensed God calling her to devote more time to serving underprivileged kids. During a mission trip to Brooklyn that summer, in which the group reached out to low-income families, she led a boy, Matthew, to the Lord. God began tugging at her heart.

When she got home, Lauren asked me one night as we were sitting on the floor in her room, "Mom, what about all the people who have never heard of Jesus? What will happen to them?"

I told her that God knows all hearts and brings the Gospel to all who seek the truth. "But He uses people to do that. That's why it's important for us to go."

At the beginning of school, her junior year, she wrote these words one Sunday at youth group, a description of what God was doing in her life:

> "I really realized that I can do things! That I can make a difference. I learned to think about the other countries. They aren't just like us, they have nothing compared to us. I am a servant of the Lord and I will do anything, go anywhere He wants me to. And I feel that He is calling

me to go somewhere that not everybody has everything they need, specifically God. A lot of people haven't heard of God and that blows me away. I hate thinking that these people might die without hearing the love of Jesus. I want to reach them."

Lauren decided not to play basketball her junior year so she could volunteer at an after-school program for kids from low-income families in Tulsa. She loved it. So when her youth minister planned a trip to Africa for the next summer, she applied immediately and began raising funds to help pay her way.

Lauren loving on kids

I was proud of my children as they grew, but don't get the crazy idea that I thought they were perfect. Jordan struggled with a lack of self-discipline, both at home and at school. This led to conflict at home, lack of effort at school, and less than truthful behavior at times. Lauren butted heads with me often in her attitude toward my authority and her growing freedom. But they were both well aware of the sin in their lives, and hated the battle they had with it. At times, I got frustrated with some of our struggles. Now I see their conviction of sin and desire to change as marks of their journeys with God that were real and a work in progress.

During these years, our youngest son, Jonathan, was still in early elementary school, the time when leading kids in a relationship with God is much simpler. He too, accepted the Gospel and prayed for salvation as a child. But I knew that he would one day have to choose an intimate relationship with Christ for himself.

Jordan left for college in the fall of 2007, trying to find the path that God had for him. He wanted to pursue his gift and love for music. In the mean-time, life at our house was different with only two children left at home. Lauren was a junior and able to drive herself and Jonathan to school every day. Two days a week they volunteered at the South Peoria House after-school care program.

All of this left me with more free time on my hands than I'd had in years. God had planted in me the vision for a discipleship ministry, and I felt like it was time to begin. So I did. Life took on a new rhythm, and we all settled in. My greatest challenge was trying to reign in my zealously compassionate daughter who still needed guidance. She wasn't always willing to listen to my wisdom.

On Sunday, February 3, 2008, our struggle came to a head. The youth ministry had planned a Super Bowl party, and Lauren invited a boy she met the previous weekend while working at AngelFood, a food ministry at our church. He was there working to help his family earn boxes of food. Several kids in the youth group befriended him and invited him to church. When Sunday arrived, Lauren heard that he needed a ride to the Super Bowl party. She offered to pick him up. Considering the area of town he lived in and the fact that she was also driving Jonathan and another young lady, Clara, I told her that she could pick the boy up—it would still be daylight. But he would have to get a ride home with an adult since it would be dark by then.

My decision didn't sit well with Lauren, and she reacted badly, losing her privilege of going to the party at all. That evening, Scott and I each had wonderful conversations with her. I was able to tell her how proud I was of her, helping her see that I didn't think she was unwise, just inexperienced. Our relationship had been a bit off track the week before, but that night turned it back in the right direction.

One week and one day later, on the morning of February 11, 2008, I saw Lauren and Jonathan off to school, then spent the day doing laundry and errands. That afternoon, as I was unloading groceries, I got a call. It was time for the kids to be home, but not late enough for me to wonder where they were. My friend Virginia told me the kids had been in an accident on a road near our home.

As I rushed out the door, my first question was "Are they ok?"

Her answer, "I don't know." I hung up and called my husband, my mind not willing to consider anything was seriously wrong.

When I neared the street on which the accident occurred, a police officer was directing traffic past the street, not allowing anyone to turn onto it. Again, my mind didn't want to consider what this could mean. I told the patrolman that my kids were the ones in the accident down the road. He waved me through. As I approached the scene, I saw my daughter's Nissan Pathfinder out in a field upside down. "No, God, NO!" I couldn't hold my dread at bay any longer.

Emergency vehicles were already there so I pulled up as close as I could, spotting Jonathan standing on the other side of the road. Relief flooded through me. I got out and ran to him, hugging him tightly. "Where's Lauren?" I asked.

Agitated, he pointed toward the car. Someone, I'm not sure who, said, "She's still out there."

My friend Virginia appeared. Another friend, Susan, who was driving behind the kids when the accident occurred, joined us. She and Virginia surrounded Jonathan and me, and we prayed desperately for Lauren. A few minutes later, my husband, Scott arrived and I ran to him. He was on the phone with our oldest son, Jordan. "Pray as you never have before," I heard him say.

Just then, a female police officer approached me. I can't remember exactly what she said, I only heard the words, "I'm sorry...accident...daughter...killed."

Pain like I had never felt before sliced through me. "NOOO!" I screamed, running to Scott's car where he was still on the phone with Jordan. All I could say was "She's gone! She's gone!"

My memories are disjointed after that. Sitting in Virginia's car with Scott and Jonathan...our friend and minister, Steve, appearing and reaching for all of us, sobbing openly...someone deciding to take us to the church. So began our journey into every parent's greatest nightmare.

The next few hours and days went by in a haze of decisions and a blur of people. So many of our friends and loved ones came to the church that first night to comfort and weep with us. Lauren's friends from school and church began to appear as they got word of the accident. Her best friends were inconsolable. Kathryn, more like Lauren's twin sister than best friend, was crying and talking hysterically about all the plans she and Lauren had made for their future. She felt completely lost. So did I.

It was in those initial hours that we first saw the hand of God move powerfully in our midst on our behalf. Both Scott and I had a supernatural strength to minister to others. Scott made his way around the ever-increasing crowd in the church sanctuary, assuring people that God was in control and that we could trust Him. My heart hurt every time another of Lauren's friends rushed to me. They clung to me tightly, their broken hearts needing comfort. My nephew Matthew, closest in age to Lauren, climbed over pews to reach me. Gut-wrenching sobs wracked him. With each new arrival, God gave me a compassion I couldn't begin to understand but for which I was so grateful.

God spoke the most comforting words we heard that night through a young man from Lauren's school. We didn't know him, but as Scott approached the group he was with, he could see the boy was weeping uncontrollably. Thinking he was expressing deep grief, Scott reached out to try to comfort him. But the young man grabbed an offering envelope, wrote on it, and handed it to Scott. "I am overwhelmed. God wants me to tell you, 'Good job. I love you.'" Overcome as he read the words spoken straight from the Father, Scott made his way over to share them with me.

Wednesday, February 13th, the church held two services—one for adults and one for the youth—to minister to our family and friends who were grieving so deeply. During the youth service, paper and pens were set out for kids to write notes to us and to Lauren. They were presented to us in a hand-made pillow with pictures of Lauren and her friends on it. The words "Love Letters to Lauren" were stitched on the front. That night at home, as I read through each one, I came across a note from one of her basketball coaches. At the bottom it said, "She's not gone, she's just gone ahead." This was my first glimmer of the hope I would need most to survive. It hinted at a new horizon God would eventually raise my eyes to see.

On Valentine's Day, 2008, we held a Celebration of Life memorial service for our precious daughter, Lauren Michelle Crawley. Shortly before we left for the church that morning, a gift arrived on our doorstep. I opened it to find a small picture of an empty tomb. This scripture was underneath: *"I am the resurrection and the life; he that believeth in me, though he were dead, yet shall he live"* (John 11:25, KJV). A second glimmer, confirming a promise God gave us two days before, preparing for the service.

We met with our ministers the day after the accident to plan Lauren's memorial service. While we were talking, my dear friend Jamie came into the room and handed me Lauren's Bible, which was among the things found in her car. I leafed through it while Scott and our ministers talked about the service. It fell open to a page and I saw before me a handmade pink bookmark. John 3:16 was printed on it with blanks where Lauren had filled in her name. "For God so loved <u>Lauren</u> that He gave His only begotten Son, that if <u>Lauren</u> believes in Him <u>Lauren</u> will not perish but have everlasting life." Even through overwhelming pain, I recognized the message God had just given me. Lauren did not perish but was with her Lord Jesus, because she believed in Him.

I held up the bookmark and silence fell over the group as they read the words on it. We immediately knew this was part of the message of Lauren's life God gave us to share at her service. Lauren's youth pastor presented the Gospel, so he used her bookmark as part of the presentation. At the end of the service, we made copies of her bookmark (with the blanks left empty) available to the 2000+ people in attendance. Since then we have been told of those who gave their hearts to the Lord that day. We have also heard from many people how God has helped them share the Gospel with Lauren's bookmark.

In the days following Lauren's accident, a blanket of darkness and silence descended on me, blocking my ability to connect with God like I had for the past seven years. My first strangled cries to Him were "God, are You there?" "I can't find You," and "please help me." He seemed so silent. After being an avid journaler in my relationship with Christ, my first journal entry after the accident was broken and disjointed: *Lord, I can't seem to write again. What happened, what I'm feeling, all my questions, even the miracles You are doing. Help*

me. That's all. I felt paralyzed, completely unable to connect with God. I couldn't pray, write, or read His Word.

This seems to be the dilemma of many believers after tragedy strikes their lives. What a greater tragedy we suffer if we never fight our way out of this paralysis. I believe it's Satan's plan to kick God's children when they're down, to make sure they are blinded to the greatest source of comfort, strength, and healing they have—the unparalleled comfort and counsel of God and His Word.

Over the next weeks, the Holy Spirit began to break through to me. You see, He wasn't really silent, I just couldn't hear Him over the roar of my pain. We received hundreds of cards, so many with scriptures in them. The ones I clung to were the promises of eternal life for God's children. God knew this was the only comfort I would be able to hear for a long time. It was the lifeline He used to begin the long process of pulling me out of the pit of grief.

> *"For we know that when this earthly tent we live in is taken down—when we die and leave these bodies—we will have a home in heaven, an eternal body made for us by God himself and not by human hands...Yes, we are fully confident, and we would rather be away from these bodies, for then we will be at home with the Lord."*

> 2 Corinthians 4:1, 8

> *"And now, brothers and sisters, I want you to know what will happen to the Christians who have died so you will not be full of sorrow like people who have no hope. For since we believe that Jesus died and was raised to life again, we*

also believe that when Jesus comes, God will bring back with Jesus all the Christians who have died... Then, together with them, we who are still alive and remain on the earth will be caught up in the clouds to meet the Lord in the air and remain with him forever."

1 Thessalonians 4:13-14, 17

"But we are citizens of heaven, where the Lord Jesus Christ lives. And we are eagerly waiting for him to return as our Savior. He will take these weak mortal bodies of ours and change them into glorious bodies like his own, using the same mighty power that he will use to conquer everything, everywhere."

Philippians 3:20-21

"Every human being has an earthly body just like Adam's, but our heavenly bodies will be just like Christ's...It will happen in a moment, in the blinking of an eye, when the last trumpet is blown. For when the trumpet sounds, the Christians who have died will be raised with transformed bodies. And then we who are living will be transformed so that we will never die."

1 Corinthians 15:48, 52

I clung to the promises that my daughter is alive and I'll one day be reunited with her *physically*, not just spiritually. I in my new body and she in hers, we'll one day embrace, never to be separated by death again. There's no greater comfort than this! And it's all true because God poured out

23

His love at the cross where His own Son died for us. He is the greatest Comforter with the greatest comfort of all. (Much more to come on God's eternal promises.)

Another incredible source of comfort came to me through Lauren's own words in her journals. She had many of them, filled with Scriptures and prayers, doodles and notes with friends, and lots of drawings and expressions of her love for Jesus. In them, I found a depth of relationship and desire for Christ-likeness that surprised me. Yet they were consistent with her growing passion and calling. As early as ninth grade, she was writing things like:

6/22/05

Lord I come to you in prayer this morning. Lord I give you my day. Help me to glorify you in all I do. Lord help me to act like you would. I want people to look at me and my actions and be able to know that I love You! You're amazing! I love you.

Sept. 8, 2005

Dear God, thank You for giving me this day. Lord I love you so much. You are the way, the truth and the life! (Light) You're so amazing. Lord I give you my day, shine through me today. Lord help me to have joy in serving other people today!

Over and over, Lauren prayed for God to flow through her and shine through her:

Shine through me. Lord help me to love everyone. Lord shine through me. I want to be like you!

I give you my day. Lord take it and use it for your will! Flow and shine through me!

The predominant scripture in her journals was Luke 9:23: *"If any of you wants to be my follower, you must put aside your selfish ambition, shoulder your cross daily and follow me."* It was often her prayer for God to take her day and make her a light for Christ at school. And she kept a list of friends whose salvation she was praying for.

Lauren's journals showed us her heart. The letters we received from her classmates in the weeks following the accident showed us the actions that matched:

Lauren was one of the few people who really made a difference in my life...Her smile brightened my day, and her laugh brightened my week.

She was precious and from what she said and did at [school] she came straight from God. She always had a smile on her face. Her radiance would light a room up...she has brought joy to many people's lives. I will never forget when we were in Spanish 1 together and she went to give Mrs. Mullican our teacher a hug like she did every day. Mrs. Mullican was sitting on her stool like everyday but this one particular day Mrs. Mullican didn't catch her and they both fell on the ground. They both sat there in front of the class laughing their heads off almost to the point of crying...Every time when she started laughing the whole class would start to laugh. Just her presence in the room gave anyone in the room a warm feeling inside...Your daughter was amazing, kind, loving, gentle, patient, all the things you want in a classmate.

In ninth grade Lauren and I were talking about church one day. I was telling her how I don't really like my church because I don't know anyone. She always talked about how great her church was and how much she loved it. She begged me to go with her that coming Sunday, so I agreed. I was really excited to hang out with her and just to see what her awesome church was like. The night before was the night she cut her leg really bad and had to get a lot of stitches. I figured that she probably wouldn't be going to church since she was on crutches and such, so I decided it best not to meet her at church that Sunday. At school on Monday, she came up to me with a smile and said, 'Where were you! I was waiting for you!' I felt so bad! I just figured that since she cut open her leg that she would miss one Sunday of church, be she didn't. She went anyway...and that utterly amazed me.

She was always smiling and laughing. I will never ever forget her laugh. She had such a gorgeous voice. We were talking in Mr. Doyle's class the other day and he was saying how Lauren stood out, and it is so true. She just glowed or something, I'm not quite sure, but she was always noticeable. I always looked up to her, ever since 6th grade. I always wanted to be her friend or her partner. She was just the kind of person that everyone wants to be around. She has been such a big impact on my life, and will continue to be.

One young woman from a different school wrote Jordan to tell him that though she never met Lauren, she attended her service with two friends who went to school with Lauren. She was deeply moved by Lauren's life. After the service, she was able to talk to one of her friends about the preciousness of life. She wrote,

> To make an incredibly long conversation short, I think Lauren Crawley saved his life…I'm telling you this because when tragic things like this happen, often times it is hard to actually grasp the reality of what truly was. Lauren changed peoples' lives. She saved them. Many more than would ever walk up to a microphone. Many more than will ever realize it. Your sister reached people that I am convinced no one else could. She even managed to reach me. A girl from a different school who she never even met.

We continued to receive notes and hear stories from her friends and people she only met once or twice. All of them gave us the same picture: a young woman lit from within by her relationship with Jesus Christ. Even three years later, I received a Facebook message from one of her basketball teammates:

> Hi Alicia, I am not one hundred percent sure that you will remember me, but I played basketball with Lauren for a couple of years at [school]…She was always such an amazing light in the room. We had many laughs in the locker room and on our road trips…I really cannot tell you how many times I've been driving, doing homework, watching TV, etc… her bright smiley face with beautiful freckles just pops in my head. I start thinking about her and how you could tell by just one look at her that the Lord was with her and in her. She is such an inspiration to me in that aspect. I love that there is a distinct difference between happiness and joy, because joy is so obviously from the Lord it is amazing. Lauren had so much joy in her life that to this day I picture her in my head in order to receive that joy whenever I am lacking it. I want to walk the walk like she did and I know that the reason I always see her face is so that I remember to walk with God…She has touched my life in so many ways and to this day she continues to change my life…I can't wait to tell Lauren myself just how much she has touched my life.

What a gift to continue to see so much evidence from Lauren's life that assures us of where she is now. We have never had a moment's doubt that she's with Jesus, not because she walked an aisle at church, prayed a prayer, or was baptized, but because she lived as one forgiven and free to love and serve her Savior.

Lauren's demeanor of joy that shone like a light on those around her was truly a work of God. When she was a little girl, she had a fun personality, but there were big streaks of a negative outlook mixed in. She tended to see the glass half empty. I remember picking her up from school one day, and her first words to me were, "Mommy, seven bad things happened to me today!" Then she proceeded to list them. Scott and I encouraged her often to see things in a more positive way, but I know it was the love of Jesus that gave her the joy she eventually exuded so freely.

God was present with us in the first moments and days of our grief, and continued to visibly comfort us through others and to work in obvious ways. Over the next three years, we would encounter Him in innumerable ways. I want to share with you how the Holy Spirit, my *Wonderful* Counselor, walked me through the darkest valley of grief I have ever traveled.

Chapter 3—Turmoil

The weeks following Lauren's home-going were filled with a sense of unreality. I didn't recognize my life anymore. I remember thinking that I felt like I had been yanked out of my life and dropped into one I couldn't make sense of and didn't belong in. As a result, it was terribly hard to function. God carried us through the first week of funeral arrangements, friends, family, and all the details we had to face. Now, we didn't know how to get back to "normal" life. How could we? Nothing would ever be normal again. My journal entries record my battle to understand life again.

2/21/2008

Lord, I'm in a lot of pain. A huge chunk of my heart has been ripped out and taken with Lauren. I'll never get it back. I will always be not quite whole until we're reunited forever. Thoughts and images of the accident haunt me. I haven't found peace in those memories yet. But the absolute knowledge that Lauren has inherited life with

You forever is starting to sink into my heart and give me peace.

My Counseling Begins

It would be a long time before that knowledge became truly real to me, because I couldn't get my head around how someone so present in my life wasn't there anymore. The "unreal-ness" of her absence made it impossible for me to understand that she was actually present with the Lord. All I could do at first was cling to the promises of God's Word until they became real to me. And they only would with time and much wise counsel.

So that is where God began with me on my journey of healing—with much wise counsel from His Word. For seven years, I had begun each day spending time with the Lord. He would speak to me through His Word and Holy Spirit, and I would respond to Him in journaling and prayer. After the accident, I didn't open my Bible or journal for almost two weeks, but soon I found I couldn't face another day of grief without them.

I can't give you any rhyme or reason for what I read. All I know is, as I waited before Him, the Holy Spirit led me to scriptures that spoke what He wanted to say to me. And there He met me in the midst of all my confusion. Some verses were in cards we received. Some were in a journal a friend gave me. Verses I connected with in any way, I explored with Him. Here's the first one:

> *"The thought of my suffering and homelessness is bitter beyond words. I will never forget this awful time, as I grieve over my loss. Yet I still dare to hope when I remember this: The unfailing*

*love of the Lord never ends! By his mercies we
have been kept from complete destruction. Great
is his faithfulness; his mercies begin afresh each
day. I say to myself, 'The Lord is my inheritance;
therefore, I will hope in him!'"*

Lamentations 3:19-24

These words described exactly what I felt, what
consumed my world now. Because I couldn't make sense
of anything I was feeling, this and other verses expressed
things I didn't even know were inside of me until I read
them. But that wasn't all they did; the scriptures God led
me to also declared the truth I needed to hear and grab hold
of. Could I "dare to hope?" I had to try. It was a matter of
life or death for me at that point. I didn't see how I would
ever be able to go on, to survive even one more day separated
from my daughter. As God spoke to me, I wrote:

2/21/2008

*Lord, Scott and I are so thankful for Your presence
and Your work during this time. Thank You for
the witness You've helped us be. But we are hurting
<u>so</u> much. It's difficult to function, to get through
the day. Help us Lord, as things get worse. Help
us to know that we can cry out in pain and grief,
sorrow and anger, without dimming Your glory
or hurting our witness. Help us to know when
it's okay for us to turn inward and deal with our
tormented thoughts, feelings and memories. Help
us to see that it's okay for us not to know how to
go on, or how to pick up the pieces and live again.
Life here seems so empty now, emptier than it's
ever been. I miss my baby so much! Tell her, Lord,*

31

*how much I love and miss her. Tell her I can't wait
to meet her at the gates of heaven.*

God spoke to me again through these verses:

*"I cried out to the Lord in my suffering, and He
heard me. He set me free from all my fears... The
Lord hears His people when they call to Him for
help. He rescues them from all their troubles. The
Lord is close to the broken-hearted; He rescues
those who are crushed in spirit."*

Psalm 34:6, 17-18

One emotion I experienced that surprised me was fear.
Grief brought so much fear with it that it blindsided me.
From the first day, I was so incredibly afraid, yet I didn't
understand it, couldn't pinpoint what it was rooted in. But
God addressed it immediately, telling me He would set me
free from fear. I'll tell you more about how He did that
in a later chapter, but I want to share one thing He did
immediately, because it's so precious to me.

My initial fear was that God wasn't there. I felt lost
and completely alone inside. I couldn't feel His presence
like I had for so long. Everything had gone dark and silent,
and I couldn't find Him. But He began to bring me verse
after verse that said, "Do not be afraid." Most of them also
promised, "I am with you" in some way. Just as a parent
quiets her child's fears by saying, "It's okay, I'm here. Don't
be afraid," so the Holy Spirit did with me, over and over. It's
what I needed from the start, and He knew it.

I realize now that God never left me. Not only was He
with me through His Spirit, but through His body, the
church, as well. So many people drew together to support

us in beautiful and amazing ways. Minutes after we found out Lauren had gone to heaven at the accident scene, one of our ministers, who is also a dear friend, was by our side weeping with us. Others arranged for us to go to the church straight from the accident site. By the time we arrived, people were showing up. As word of the accident spread, Lauren's friends, teammates, teachers and coaches came, along with our family, friends, school administrators, ministers and neighbors. The church was soon filled with people who loved our daughter and us.

In the days that followed, friends filled our home, ministering to us and our extended family in different ways. They arranged meals, gathered pictures to be shown at Lauren's service, answered the phone, did laundry, cleaned, and did just about everything else it takes to survive. This continued for months. Just like Paul says, *"If one part [of the body] suffers, all the parts suffer with it"* (1 Corinthians 12:26). We saw this so clearly in the body of Christ through our deepest grief.

But even though we found much comfort through our church family in those first hours, weeks and months, I continued to struggle with a sense of dark aloneness inside. Everything in me cried out to hear God, to know He was there. There was so much turmoil inside of me that I couldn't sort it out alone. I prayed over and over for God to give me His peace. Repeatedly, He gave me scriptures that strongly exhorted me to hold on tightly to Christ, to come to Him with everything. He spoke:

> *"But you must remain faithful to the things you have been taught. You know they are true, for you can trust those who taught you. You have been taught the holy Scriptures from childhood,*

and they have given you the wisdom to receive the salvation that comes by trusting in Christ Jesus."

2 Timothy 3:14-15

"Without wavering, let us hold tightly to the hope we say we have, for God can be trusted to keep His promise...Do not throw away this confident trust in the Lord, no matter what happens."

Hebrews 10:23, 35

I responded:

3/6/2008

God gave me these words commanding me to hold on to what I know, and not to throw out everything He has planted in my heart. When I'm tempted to jump ship, thinking to save myself from the agony of shaken faith, God tells me to stay in the boat. I'm to remain faithful to the things I've been taught, not to throw away this confident trust in the Lord, no matter what happens. I must hold tightly to the hope I say I have, for <u>He can be trusted</u> to keep His promise. If I jump now to "save" myself, I will perish instead. This is exactly what Satan wants me to do. But God can be trusted, and I must stay with Him in the boat, even when I feel thrown around by the massive waves of circumstance. I'm safe with Him and <u>only</u> with Him. Jesus, my only comfort, peace, and sanity is in You—in Your character and Your promises. I don't know how I'll ever get through the rest of my life here. But I'm convinced that the only place for me to be is in *the boat with you, clinging to You each day, one day at a time. Please Lord, when I'm tempted to jump ship, pull me away from the edge and hold me in Your arms of love. You are my only peace in the midst of this storm, as turmoil rages inside of me. Calm my heart and mind. Help me to find peace and rest in You.*

He spoke:

"But we worship at your throne—eternal, high and glorious! O Lord, the hope of Israel, all who turn away from you will be disgraced and shamed. They will be buried in a dry and dusty grave, for they have forsaken the Lord, the fountain of living water. O Lord, you alone can heal me; you alone can save. My praises are for you alone!"

Jeremiah 17:12-14

I responded:

3/7/2008

I will not forsake the Lord or the truth I've been taught. He alone is the living water. May this be me: "Blessed are those who trust in the Lord, and have made the Lord their hope and confidence. They are like trees planted along a riverbank, with roots that reach deep into the water. Such trees are not bothered by the heat or drought. Their leaves stay green, and they go right on producing delicious fruit" (Jeremiah 17:7-8).

Over and over I turned to His Word, pouring out my heart on paper, and listening for Him to speak. And He did speak. Abundantly. I heard, I wrote, I cried, and I prayed. Little by little, He sorted out my confusion and spoke truth to me.

Whether you have spent much time in God's Word or not, you may be saying, "That's well and good for you, Alicia, but I have no idea how to start or where to turn."

I confess that, even though I had been in fellowship with the Lord in His Word for years, I too, was at a complete loss. But our God knows and understands us so well. He'll meet you right where you are—all you have to do is ask Him. He may send someone to help you get started, He may get a book into your hands that points the way, or He may be present with you in a way you can sense the first time you open the Word on your own. He loves you and He knows how to reach you when you're willing.

When I felt like I was drowning in grief, the Holy Spirit brought scripture to me. Certain verses on the cards we received spoke to me. My journal had scriptures in it. Friends gave me passages of hope and comfort. The verses above, Jeremiah 17:7-8, were given to me by my friend Karen on the very same day I read Psalm 1. Both passages use virtually the same words. Watch for those things. They're not coincidence. They are the Holy Spirit speaking to you. Listen and respond, and He'll draw you to His side, counseling you with His wisdom. It far exceeds that of any human counselor.

Please don't think I'm against other sources of help. I read my share of books on grief. But I always tried to look for ones with a biblical perspective. The Holy Spirit used many scriptures in those books written by wise and godly people traveling the road ahead of me. They shared them from their own journey with God through tragedy and sorrow. Though God didn't lead me to seek professional counseling, He may prompt you to do so. A wise and godly counselor can help you connect with God and His Word, pointing you to the Wonderful Counselor.

Hold Tightly to the Truth

From the turmoil of my first excruciating days of grief, the Holy Spirit called me tenderly yet firmly to hold tightly to Him. He assured me everything I knew was true. And He showed me that what's true in the light doesn't stop being true when it gets dark. Here's the picture He gave me:

4/11/2008

> *It would be like seeing all the furniture in my bedroom during the day: I walk around it, sit on it, and set things on it. But then I begin to doubt it's still there at night, just because I can't see it anymore. I wouldn't do that; what I do instead is continue to walk around it, lie on my bed, and reach for things on my nightstand <u>in the dark</u>. If I thought the furniture wasn't there just because I could no longer see it, I would crash into it. I would find another place to sleep, and wouldn't be able to find things I set on it. It wouldn't be rational to do that.*

The same goes for the truth. What I knew of the Lord Jesus Christ as I walked in the light of a growing, passionate love relationship with Him was still true in my darkest hour. When I couldn't see the truth, I had to believe and act like it was still the truth. Did I believe in my glorious God *"who is able to keep you from stumbling, and who will bring you into his glorious presence, innocent of sin and with great joy"* (Jude 24)? Even though He didn't always *feel* true in my pain, confusion and turmoil, I had to decide if I was going to believe He *was* true, or jump ship. The Holy Spirit helped me see that jumping ship wasn't an option if I wanted to survive.

So how was I to survive? One day, exactly two weeks after Lauren went to heaven, my time with the Lord began with these simple words: *"I weep with grief; encourage me by Your Word"* (Psalm 119:28).

2/25/2008

Lord, I need You in a personal and intimate way. So far, You have loved, comforted and helped us through people—the body of Christ. And it's been amazing. But on the inside, the pain is so great that I can't feel anything else. It's so loud that I'm having trouble hearing Your voice. Please, please encourage me by Your Word today, by Your voice speaking to me. I need to feel You inside. I need to know Your presence and to have the flame of passion for You ignited again.

I knew I had to keep going to God's Word, the Truth, if I had any chance of surviving. And I had to hear and feel the Holy Spirit inside of me again. Hearing came almost from the beginning. But it would be much longer before I felt Him again. There was so much pain, turmoil, fear and confusion that if I hadn't clung to the Word like a bulldog, I don't think I would have ever made it back to intimacy with God.

There were times I wanted to give up and walk away. But I had nowhere else to go. When the crowds started to desert Jesus after they realized He wasn't what they wanted,

Jesus asked His disciples: *"Are you going to leave, too?"* Peter's answer was my answer: *"Lord, to whom would we go? You alone have the words that give eternal life. We believe them and we know you are the Holy One of God"* (see John 6:66-69).

2/25/2008

"Oh that you would burst from the heavens and come down!...For since the world began, no ear has heard, and no eye has seen a God like you, who works for those who wait for Him! You welcome those who cheerfully do good, who follow godly ways. But we are not godly...When we proudly display our righteous deeds, we find they are but filthy rags...And yet, Lord, you are our Father. We are the clay, and you are the potter."

Isaiah 64:1, 4, 8

Lord, keep me close, don't let me turn away, don't let my heart get hard. Remind me of who You are, that I may continue to fear You, even as I question and process all that's happened. Thank You for reminding me that there is no God like You. You are the Potter, I am the clay. Help me to submit to Your ways concerning me. Forgive me for "displaying my righteous deeds," for I've found that "they are but filthy rags."

The Blame Game

A sense of guilt and failure caused much of the turmoil in my heart. I now understand why people blame themselves endlessly when tragedy strikes, even when it's not rational.

Guilt haunted me for asking Lauren to stop and pick up a vacuum cleaner from Scott's office. Leaving the office, she was on the phone as she got back in the car. As a result, she failed to put her seatbelt back on. I was convinced she would have been okay if she'd had it on, and she would have had it on if I hadn't asked her to stop.

Scott blamed himself because it was his decision to let her drive an SUV—it had a rollover warning. Jonathan blamed himself because he saw that Lauren's seatbelt wasn't buckled, and he failed to tell her. And that was only the beginning. Scott and I second-guessed many decisions we made, as far back as moving across town two and a half years before. This was the reason Lauren was driving on the road where the accident happened.

As the weeks went by, every argument I'd ever had with Lauren paraded through my mind. I judged every parenting decision I made and came up lacking: words I said, and frustration I expressed to her, Scott and God. I decided that God took her because I was failing as a parent.

To top off my self-blame, losing a child felt like a failure in itself. It's a mother's job to protect her children and get them safely to adulthood. I failed to do that, and I blamed myself. Over time, with the Holy Spirit's help and some honest conversations with my husband, I saw that Lauren's home-going wasn't a change in God's plans for her in order to punish me. There's a scripture in Psalm 139 that helps many grieving parents who feel they have failed their child. The whole chapter reminds us of God's intimate involvement in each and every life. Then verse 16 says this: *"You saw me before I was born. Every day of my life was recorded in your book. Every moment was laid out before a single day had passed."*

Why So Brief?

Initially, it was very painful for me to think that, from before Lauren was born, she was only meant to be here less than seventeen years. When we held her for the first time, God already knew those few years were all He had planned for her here. That hurt. But in His infinite patience, God led me to a difficult but precious truth.

When a child dies, people often ask: *Why would God bring a child into the world to live such a short time? What is the purpose of that life, and why cause so much pain from the loss?* These questions show that we fail to see two things.

One, God uses *every* life for good, even babies who are miscarried, stillborn or aborted. God invites those affected by these tragedies to see Him and draw close to Him through it. Broken by the harsh reality of life in this fallen world, some will seek Him for answers. As they look to Him for what the world can't provide, they are changed, for His glory and their good.

Two, *everyone* is created to live forever. We choose either to be with God, eternally alive, or without God, eternally punished (see Daniel 12:2, Matthew 25:46). A baby may only live two months here on earth or he may not live here even one day. But because God is merciful to those who never had the knowledge or chance to trust Christ for salvation, that child will live forever with the Lord. My daughter lived less than seventeen years here; some would consider that a waste. But her life is no shorter than my 97-year old grandmother's. They will both live forever with Jesus because they're His children by faith. One just stayed on earth longer than the other.

Nancy Guthrie, who released two infants to heaven, says it like this:

"We tend to think this life on earth is all there is, and we certainly live that way much of the time. God wants to radically alter that perspective. He wants us to live with an eternal perspective, putting life on this earth in its proper place and living in anticipation of an eternity in his presence. If we really believe that true life, fullness of joy, and freedom from pain are found in an eternity in God's presence, why do we cling to this earthly life with such vigor?...There is no tragedy in being ushered quickly from this life to the next when that next life is spent in the presence of God. There is nothing to fear. The only real tragedy is a life that ends without the hope of eternal life in the presence of God... Do you find yourself yearning for heaven in the midst of your sorrow or difficulty? Perhaps that is part of the purpose in your pain—a new perspective, a proper perspective, about life on this earth and the life after."[2]

Question Carefully

In all of my turmoil and questioning, I knew that if I was truly going to hang on to my faith, I had to remember that God is God. Otherwise there would be no reason to keep turning to Him. So there were lines I couldn't cross. Yes, I could cry out to God. Yes, I could question His ways. I could even express my doubts to Him, pound on His chest, and beg to have Lauren back. But there was one thing I couldn't do.

---

[2] Nancy Guthrie, *Holding on to Hope* (Carol Stream, IL: Tyndale House Publishers, Inc., 2002), 58-59.

In the book of Job, Job brought his questions to God, declaring his innocence before Him. This was true in a sense, and Job defended his innocence to his less-than-helpful friends. But he also convinced himself that since he hadn't knowingly sinned, God owed him an explanation for the tragedy that struck his life.

> *"Let the Almighty show me that I am wrong. Let my accuser write out the charges against me. I would face the accusation proudly. I would treasure it like a crown. For I would tell him exactly what I have done. I would come before him like a prince."*

> Job 31:35b-37

Job seemed quite sure he had a strong case against God—until God answered with a few questions of His own. Four chapters of questions. Job's only reply was, *"I was talking about things I did not understand, things far too wonderful for me...I take back everything I said, and I sit in dust and ashes to show my repentance"* (Job 42:3b, 6). Though Job was a righteous man and could list chapters full of his good deeds, he was still a sinner. So am I. Job, a mere human, had no grounds to *demand* an answer from God about what was happening in his life. Neither do I. God didn't *owe* Job an explanation. And He doesn't owe me one.

Does this mean I shouldn't ask God for understanding or bring Him my desperate, heart-broken questions? Not at all. It just means that I must never demand that God answer to me. He is the Potter, I am the clay. My righteous acts are like filthy rags before Him. I could never be innocent enough to face Him proudly and argue over His ways. Coming to

God like this shows that I just want to defend myself before Him, not truly understand His ways.

But when I come to Him in humility and brokenness, recognizing His rightful sovereignty over all He has made, He meets me there. Sometimes with greater insight into His ways. Sometimes with a better understanding of the big picture. *Always* with tender mercy, a Father's love, and a little more healing.

And so I sought God relentlessly, receiving insight when He chose to give it, and trying to rest in the comfort of His presence when my questions went unanswered. What I found is that God wanted to give me many more answers than what I'd been led to believe. So often, when something devastating happens, we're told that we'll never understand it, this side of heaven.

"Remember," people say, "God's thoughts 'are completely different from yours.' His 'ways are far beyond anything you could imagine'" (see Isaiah 55:8). And this is true.

But God has been abundant in making the mysteries of His eternal plan so much more visible to me than I ever thought possible. How? *"We know these things because God has revealed them to us **by his Spirit**, and his Spirit searches out everything and shows us even God's deep secrets"* (1 Corinthians 2:10). We may not be able to imagine or understand God's ways on our own, but through His Spirit living in us, He does reveal some of His mysteries to us. And most of those revelations come through the difficult things in life. They are part of His counsel.

Chapter 4—Hope: Heaven and the Restoration of all Things

I was so excited to write this chapter! Reunion with Lauren was the first promise the Holy Spirit gave me, and I'm so thankful to Him for that. For it's the hope of God's eternal promises that restored my joy in this life. I believe it's the only source of hope and joy that the brokenness of this world can't steal or destroy. Thank You, Jesus, for making all things new!

No matter what troubles you've faced, or will face, in this life, the promise of God, *"Look, I am making all things new!"* (Revelation 21:5) is for you. It may be grief over a loved one's death, a divorce, health problems, a financial crisis, or just the weariness of life's disappointments. God's promise to make all things new means that a whole new kind of world is coming, one without death, sorrow, crying or pain of any kind. For those who put their faith in Christ, God is preparing the life He always intended us to have. So whether you are mourning the death of a person, relationship, dream, or plan, look ahead to the new life Jesus came to give. He, and it, will never disappoint.

Thankfully, before the accident, my passion for Jesus and my desire to see Him face to face drove me to learn some things about heaven. After the accident, I had to know everything about Lauren's new home. I wanted to be able to picture all I possibly could about it. And so I searched, reading everything Scripture says about heaven. I looked at what Bible scholars have written on the subject. I needed more understanding and perspective on the truth about eternal life.

We'd already gotten a few glimpses of Lauren's new life: "She's not gone, she's just gone ahead." "*I am the resurrection and the life. Those who believe in me…are given eternal life for believing in me and will never perish.*" But now it was time to get serious and really learn about that life. I had to, to survive.

Before Jordan left home for college, I learned everything I could about where he was going. When he moved there, I went with him to help him move in. I wanted to be able to picture where my "little" boy now lived, since he was no longer under our roof. When Lauren left home for heaven, I did the same thing. My friend Alisa tells me that for the first year, I "took care of Lauren," making sure she was alright. It's true. I had to know my baby girl was safe, happy, and well-cared for.

3/28/2008

Missing Lauren

Lord, I really miss my baby girl. It's so hard to endure this separation, not knowing how long it will be. I give myself to You today, all of me. Carry me through one day at a time. Teach me a new way to live, give me a permanent way of

*thinking: focused on You, on heaven, on the reality
and wonderful expectation of being reunited with
Lauren forever..."He'll come down from heaven
and the dead in Christ will rise—they'll go
first. Then the rest of us who are still alive at the
time will be caught up in the clouds to meet the
Master. Oh we'll be walking on air! And then
there will be one huge family reunion with the
Master. So reassure one another with these words"*
(1 Thessalonians 4:16-18, MSG).

I needed the reassurance of those words so badly.

I want to start with what I learned about where Lauren
is now. You see, I discovered that the Bible speaks of eternal
life in two ways: life in God's presence immediately after
believers die, and life at Christ's return, in the new heavens
and new earth. They're both wonderful, but they're different.
And God's Word gives us some hints of what they'll be
like.

An Inaccurate Picture?

I think the reason most believers don't understand the
difference between where we'll go when we die and where
we'll live forever is because we don't even know they're
different. We don't know what the Bible says about them.
Neither concept is well-understood today, so the lines
between the two often get blurred. Sadly, it seems that most
of us get our "theology" about heaven from books, movies,
and other popular media. Add to this how little the church
today teaches on life after death, and what do you get? A
very foggy and unexciting mess. Truth be told, we don't
think about it much because we don't want to.

Most people, even in our modern, scientific age, still believe in some sort of afterlife. The problem is that Christians have a very vague and pieced-together idea of what it will be like. I grew up with just such a picture of heaven. You probably have a similar one: Our souls go to heaven after we die to live in a world that is completely incomprehensible to us. It isn't even physical, we think. So what will life be like there? Will we see anyone else? Will we remember who we are or recognize others? And what will we do all day? Sit on clouds and play harps?

No wonder we don't want to think about heaven. It's not very appealing, is it? In fact, many of us, if that's what we believe, aren't very excited about going there, though we'd never say it out loud. But people in heaven today aren't floating around alone and invisible, wondering who they are. And they're not unconscious. As unappealing as our idea of heaven may be, it's not a very logical picture, either. Steve Berger says it like this:

> "We do not believe that God went to all the trouble of saving us and giving us eternal life just to take us to be with Him in Heaven and then bore us to death for the rest of eternity. Might there be resting, might there be some leisurely harp playing? Sure! But there's also a lot of heart-pumping, meaningful activity in Heaven. Some people get nervous when we ascribe real living to eternal life, but if our concept of eternal life doesn't mean eternal living, then we're missing the point."[3]

---

[3]   Steve and Sarah Berger, *Have Heart: bridging the gulf between heaven and earth* (Franklin, TN: Grace Chapel, Inc., 2010), 73-74.

Maybe we would look forward to eternal life if we understood that it's not eternal retirement. Heaven isn't a rest home we go to after we've finished living. It's the life we were all meant for, yet can't experience here on earth because of the curse of sin. The "rest" of heaven is the rest we enter here when we turn to Christ and stop trying to reach God by our own efforts. It's the end of our restlessness, and one day it will be the end of the curse that makes life here such a struggle.

Eternal life isn't a halfway existence of endless inactivity and eternal boredom. And it's not a never-ending church service or sing-a-long. Yes, we'll worship our Savior continuously in heaven. But we'll express it in *everything* we do, from singing to serving to learning to exploring, our hearts completely at rest in Christ's presence.

We also won't experience eternal life in isolation. So many times, people—myself included—think of being in heaven alone. With God, yes, but what does that really mean? And being in His presence without other people seems a bit frightening. Maybe we think like this because everyone goes through the experience of death alone, leaving everything we know behind. But many Old Testament scriptures speak of the new heavens and new earth as a place where God will gather His people *together* out of every nation. They'll come together with joyous singing, dancing and feasting. They'll be reunited, the gloom of death removed forever (see Isaiah 25:6-8, 40:5, 43:5-7, 35:10 and 51:11, Jeremiah 31:10-13). Though these promises were partially and temporarily fulfilled for the nation of Israel in the Old Testament, they will not be complete until Christ returns and gathers all His people together. Jesus speaks of this very thing:

> *"And I tell you this, that many Gentiles will come from all over the world and sit down with Abraham, Isaac, and Jacob at the feast in the Kingdom of Heaven."*

Matthew 8:11

> *"And they will see the Son of Man arrive on the clouds of heaven with power and great glory. And He will send forth His angels with the sound of a mighty trumpet blast, and they will gather together His chosen ones from the farthest ends of the earth and heaven."*

Matthew 24:30b-31

Does this sound like we will be alone in heaven? No, it sounds like a party to me! Everything the Bible says about God's eternal Kingdom sounds like a joyous celebration of our King and His people. We will worship and serve Him together forever.

In the year before Lauren's accident, I learned some amazing things about heaven and the life Jesus died to give us. Most believers know that their souls will one day be in heaven with the Lord. But Jesus' death did so much more than this. I learned that, because of His resurrection, when Christ returns, the bodies of His followers will be resurrected to be like His risen body. He will create a new heavens and new earth that will be completely physical. We'll live in an eternal universe *far beyond* anything we can imagine, instead of in one we can't imagine at all. There will be continuation of our lives and relationships here, and they'll finally be perfect.

I had at least an idea of the truth—that I'd be physically reunited with my daughter one day in a relationship that will last forever. It was my first hope that I might survive my grief with a shred of sanity. This taste made me hungry for everything the Holy Spirit could teach me from God's Word about our life to come. First, though, I want to share what I learned about Lauren's life now, as a believer who died before Christ's return.

Between Death and the Resurrection

When Christ returns, He'll raise all believers to life in resurrected bodies to live forever in His restored creation. We'll look at that in a moment. But what happens to believers who die before then? The list of scriptural truths presented here are beautifully collected and documented more completely in a paper written by Judson B. Palmer, entitled "The Child of God Between Death and the Resurrection."[4]

Physical death is the separation of the soul and body. When Adam and Eve sinned in the Garden, God punished them with physical death. We inherited a sinful nature from them, and our own sin condemns us to death as well. But our souls are non-physical, living on after the body dies. The Bible teaches this, and there is a wealth of human experience, along with a growing body of scientific data, that point to it as well.

Dallas Willard, in *The Divine Conspiracy*, talks about a common human experience that's been observed frequently

---

[4]   Judson B. Palmer, *The Child of God Between Death and the Resurrection,* bibleteacher.org, http://www.woundedheart.org/cog-bda.htm, January 23, 2009.

by people as their loved ones or patients approached death. He uses allegories to describe it:

> "Another picture is of one who walks to a doorway between rooms. While still interacting with those in the room she is leaving she begins to see and converse with people in the room beyond, who may be totally concealed from those left behind. Before the widespread use of heavy sedation, it was quite common for those keeping watch to observe something like this. The one making the transition often begins to speak to those who have gone before. They come to meet us while we are still in touch with those left behind. The curtains part for us briefly before we go through."[5]

In *Beyond Death: Exploring the Evidence for Immortality*, authors Gary Habermas and J.P. Moreland give an in-depth presentation of near-death experiences (NDEs). They present current studies and write: "Studies since [the time of early popular accounts] have become much more empirical and scientific. These more recent data have effectively challenged...alternative explanations and, therefore, presented strong evidence for at least a minimalistic view of life after death."[6] The book cites several NDE testimonies that are supported by outside evidence, greatly strengthening their reliability.

---

[5]   Dallas Willard, *The Divine Conspiracy: Rediscovering Our Hidden Life in God* (San Francisco: HarperSanFrancisco, 1997), 87.

[6]   Gary Habermas, J.P Moreland, *Beyond Death: Exploring the Evidence for Immortality* (Eugene, OR: Wipf and Stock Publishers, 1998), 156.

Scripture, of course, contains the most detailed teaching about what awaits a believer when he dies. In 2 Corinthians 5, Paul says, *"For we know that when this earthly tent we live in is taken down—when we die and leave these bodies—we will have a home in heaven, an eternal body made for us by God himself and not by human hands"* (v. 1). We will leave our earthly bodies behind as they die, only to be present in heaven with Christ.

Immediately upon death, the child of God will be in the presence of the Lord. The Bible is clear about this: *"As long as we live in these bodies we are not at home with the Lord…Yes, we are fully confident, and we would rather be away from these bodies, for then we will be at home with the Lord"* (2 Corinthians 5: 6, 8). *"That is why we live by believing and not by seeing"* (v. 7). Paul also writes: *"For to me, living means living for Christ, and dying is even better…I'm torn between two desires: I long to go and be with Christ, which would be far better for me. But for your sakes, it is better that I continue to live"* (Philippians 1:21, 23-24).

In the dark days after Lauren went Home to Jesus, I had to live by believing and not by seeing. I still do. In order to survive, I had to cling to the promise that, at the very moment we were receiving the news of Lauren's physical death, she was standing in the presence of her Lord Jesus Christ. That was the picture I held onto, instead of the memories of death and destruction from that day.

3/20/2008

"Can anything ever separate us from Christ's love? Does it mean He no longer loves us if we have trouble or calamity, or are persecuted, or are hungry or cold or in danger or threatened with

death?...No, despite all these things, overwhelming victory is ours through Christ who loved us. And I am convinced that nothing can ever separate us from His love. Death can't and life can't."

Romans 8:35, 37-39

Lauren's death did not separate her from God's love. It didn't mean God stopped loving her. What it did was bring her closer to Him, perfected and whole in His presence. She's full of more life than she ever was here. Who she was here is a shadow of who she is now.

Our separation from her for this life also doesn't indicate that God no longer loves us. "Does it mean God no longer loves us?...No." Because even in death, "victory is ours through Christ who loved us." What I see from my perspective is a long and painful separation from Lauren. What God sees is a momentary interruption in an eternal relationship between us.

Jesus, please fill my heart and mind with truth as You know it. Fill me with Your thoughts and understanding concerning my eternal relationship with Lauren. Hold me close in Your arms today, for the pain is unbearable at times. I'm having so much trouble accepting that she's no longer in this life. And without the promise of eternity with her, I wouldn't make it through this at all. Draw me close to You today, Jesus. I need a vibrant, personal relationship with You, one that's full of communication with You. Remind me over and

54

over that "[You] will never fail [me], [You] will never forsake [me]. The Lord is my helper, so I will not be afraid" (Hebrews 13:5-6).

"Death is swallowed up in victory. O death, where is your victory? O death, where is your sting?"

1 Corinthians 54-55

Praise You, Lord Jesus! You purchased victory for Your children over death. Jesus, You were victorious over Lauren's physical death, raising her to eternal life with You. She is safe with You, victorious over death. Now Jesus, please make me victorious over death even now while I'm still alive on this earth. Don't let death defeat me. I love You, Lord Jesus. I am Yours, in this life and forever.

Will the child of God have a body between death and the resurrection? There are different schools of thought, but it boils down to this: we don't really know. Scripture is not completely clear on it, though inferences can be drawn. Paul says in 2 Corinthians 5:

"We grow weary in our present bodies, and we long for the day when we will put on our heavenly bodies like new clothing. For we will not be spirits without bodies, but we will put on new heavenly bodies. Our dying bodies make us groan and sigh, but it's not that we want to die and have no bodies at all. We want to slip into our new bodies so that these dying bodies will be swallowed up by everlasting life."

v. 3-4

This seems to say that Paul believed he would slip out of his dying body right into a new body. Yet we also know that our eternal bodies will be resurrected—glorified versions of our original bodies. They remain in the grave until Christ returns (more about this in a moment). So, could he be talking about some sort of transitional form of a body? After all, we were created as both physical and non-physical beings, and we will be again when Christ returns. We express ourselves and relate to the world through a physical body, and we just may do that between death and the resurrection.

Paul expresses a universal human sense of discomfort about being a spirit without a body. He indicates that He believes we won't be that at death (see passage above). And there are other scriptures that may indicate those who die in Christ have a type of glorified body. Moses and Elijah appeared in bodily form with Jesus when He was transfigured on the mountain (see Matthew 17:1-3). John, in Revelation 7, sees a *"vast crowd, too great to count, from every nation and tribe and people and language, standing in front of the throne and before the Lamb. They were clothed in white and held palm branches in their hands"* (v. 9). It's obvious he saw the bodies of people with nationalities, clothes and hands. Jesus Himself ascended to heaven in His resurrected body. I tend to believe that those in heaven now have some sort of body. But no one knows for sure.

The child of God will be conscious between death and the resurrection. Death only touches the body, not the person. We go right on living a life continued from our life on earth. Because we all have painful memories of life on earth, some people think we won't remember our past life here. But our memories are not wiped clean; instead, they are enhanced and sanctified. Several things in Scripture tell us this.

First, our painful memories are so because we don't understand God's ways. Everything hasn't been completed for our ultimate good and God's glory. When we stand before Christ, we'll be made complete in character, and He'll be able to show us so much more of His big picture. We'll see those painful memories in light of His healing and redemption. Our memories will also cause us to exalt God even higher for the way He changes our mourning into dancing. The joy He gives us in heaven will be made so much sweeter from having experienced sorrow in this life. We'll receive back all we've lost and so much more (see Matthew 19:29). I believe that our just God will heal other bad memories by taking us through a process of reconciliation with believers that we've hurt or been hurt by. All will be dealt with and forgiven in complete honesty and truth.

Second, Paul comforts believers in 1 Thessalonians 4 with the assurance of being reunited with loved ones who die in the Lord:

> *"God will bring back with Jesus all the Christians who have died…Then, **together with them**, we who are still alive and remain on the earth will be caught up in the clouds to meet the Lord in the air and remain with Him forever. So comfort and encourage each other with these words."*

> v. 14, 17-18

What comfort would this be in times of grief if we lost all memory of ourselves or others at death? It's very obvious that Paul planned on remembering the Thessalonian believers when he said earlier in the letter: *"Yes, you will bring us much joy as we stand together before our Lord Jesus when he comes back again"* (v. 19b).

Third, Revelation speaks of heaven's inhabitants worshiping the Lamb in this way: *"The Lamb is worthy—the Lamb who was killed. He is worthy to receive power and riches and wisdom and strength and honor and glory and blessing"* (5:12). Remembering the suffering and sacrifice of Christ is crucial to our worship, now and forever.

Fourth, Revelation also shows martyrs crying out to God for justice: *"O Sovereign Lord, holy and true, how long will it be before you judge the people who belong to this world for what they have done to us? When will you avenge our blood against these people?" (6:10)* They clearly have memories of their own persecution. But they remember it in light of the justice they will soon receive from the Lord.

Finally, we can look at the story of the rich man and Lazarus (possibly not a parable because it contains a named character). It gives us some clues about our state after death. We should be careful not to go too far in making parallels, but I believe we can see some things Jesus included as part of the lesson He was teaching with this story. Jesus wanted those who heard it to see that wealth does not equal righteousness, just as poverty does not equal wickedness. Lazarus the beggar went to heaven, not the selfish rich man. Abraham revealed why to the rich man using the man's own memory: *"Son, **remember** that during your lifetime you had everything you wanted, and Lazarus had nothing"* (Luke 16:25).

The rich man didn't argue with this because he *did* remember. It wasn't his wealth that condemned him; it was that he hadn't blessed others with his wealth. He also remembered something else: his brothers. *"Please, Father Abraham, send [Lazarus] to my father's home. For I have five brothers, and I want him to warn them about this place of torment so they won't have to come here when they die*" (v. 27). Obviously, the rich man still loved his brothers, showing that his life and consciousness after death was a continuation of his earthly life.

One precious inference can be made from this story as well. "If this man in torment still loved his brothers, how much more will the redeemed in Glory with Christ love those whom they loved in the flesh."[7] I believe with all my heart that Lauren remembers and loves me, her father and brothers, her loved ones, and her friends. I know she misses us, not in a sorrowful way, but in great anticipation of the day we'll be with her in the presence of Jesus. Will she even have the privilege of being beside us when we meet Him face to face? How like the Father to give her that joy!

The child of God between death and resurrection will be active and engaged. In Revelation 7:9, we find:

> *"After this I saw a vast crowd, too great to count, from every nation and tribe and people and language, standing in front of the throne and before the Lamb. They were clothed in white and held palm branches in their hands. And they were shouting with a mighty shout, 'Salvation comes from our God on the throne and from the Lamb!'"*

Whether this is all the saints of God who have died or ones who died after suffering through a specific time of tribulation, it's still God's people in heaven before the return of Christ. They're worshiping God for their salvation in the company of the angels and elders.

I also believe we'll learn, explore and discover for all eternity. God made us that way; the vastness of the universe

---

[7]   Palmer, 5.

beckons to us even now. How much more when we have all eternity to seek its wonders in our glorified bodies? And we'll never get to the end of all there is to discover about the infinite nature of our Creator.

Life for the children of God between death and the return of Christ is more wonderful than this life. The apostle Paul understood this. Even with the work of God's Kingdom still pulling at him, he knew that "to die is gain" (see Philippians 1:21-23). We may not be able to comprehend all its wonders, but a sin-free life in the presence of Jesus is much fuller and more satisfying than even the best of moments here. Yet, just like us, our loved ones in heaven now long for an even greater place: the new heavens and the new earth.

Full, Not Partial, Redemption

When God created the heavens and the earth in Genesis 1, He called all He had made "good." He called mankind—a spiritual *and* physical creation—"very good." God gave Adam and Eve meaningful work and intimate relationship with Himself and each other. All of this was set in place before the Fall. God doesn't see His physical creation or meaningful work as bad. In fact, before the Fall they were good, and part of His perfect plan. But as we know, those idyllic days didn't last. With Adam and Eve's sin, death and a curse fell over all creation.

God had a plan, though. He designed it before He created the world, knowing He would have to restore His creation to perfection. It was the plan of salvation through the suffering, death, and physical resurrection of His own beloved Son, Jesus. And He began to reveal it the very day death entered the world. Jesus' victory secured the spiritual and physical salvation of all who believe, and of all creation.

If God's plan was only to secure salvation for the souls of men and not for the rest of His good creation, Satan would win a partial victory. God and Satan would be equals, dividing the "spoils" of battle. But Satan is a created being, far inferior to his Creator. Christ's death and resurrection secured total victory. That's why modern belief falls far short of God's revealed plan in Scripture. Christ didn't go to the Cross only to make a way for our souls to go to heaven when we die. Merely helping us "escape" the cursed physical world wasn't enough for Him.

So let's explore what the Bible says Jesus won with His death and resurrection.

The New Heavens and New Earth

Let's look first at the eternal home Jesus told His disciples that He was going to prepare for them and all His followers.

> *"Don't be troubled. You trust God, now trust in Me. There are many rooms in my Father's home, and I am going to prepare a place for you. If this were not so, I would tell you plainly. When everything is ready, I will come and get you, so that you will always be with me where I am."*

> John 14:1-3

In Revelation, this place is called the new Jerusalem, and it will descend from heaven to be established on the new earth. I learned as I studied that many Bible scholars believe this will be a *renewed* heaven and earth; just like the body will die and be resurrected, so will the created universe. Both will happen when Christ returns to judge mankind and set up His Kingdom.

Peter tells us what the early church knew about Christ's return to earth:

> *"But the day of the Lord will come as unexpectedly as a thief. Then the heavens will pass away with a terrible noise, and everything in them will disappear in fire, and the earth and everything on it will be exposed to judgment...But we are looking forward to the new heavens and new earth he has promised, a world where everyone is right with God."*

> 2 Peter 3:10, 13

Out of the ashes of destruction, Christ will raise up a new and indestructible heaven and earth, just as He'll raise us on that day. How did the early church know this? Where is that promise given in the Hebrew Scriptures?

> *"Look! I am creating new heavens and a new earth—so wonderful that no one will even think about the old ones anymore. Be glad; rejoice forever in my creation! And look! I will create Jerusalem as a place of happiness. Her people will be a source of joy. I will rejoice in Jerusalem and delight in my people. And the sound of weeping and crying will be heard no more."*

> Isaiah 65:17-19

The new Jerusalem is described more in Isaiah 60:

"No longer will you need the sun or moon to give you light, for the Lord your God will be your everlasting light and he will be your glory. The sun will never set; the moon will not go down. For the Lord will be your everlasting light. Your days of mourning will come to an end."

v. 19-20

The author of Hebrews shares the hope of Abraham and others for a "heavenly city":

"Abraham did this because he was confidently looking forward to a city with eternal foundations, a city designed and built by God."

Hebrews 11:10

And:

"All these faithful ones died without receiving what God had promised them, but they saw it all from a distance and welcomed the promises of God. They agreed that they were no more than foreigners and nomads here on earth…they were looking for a better place, a heavenly homeland. That is why God is not ashamed to be called their God, for he has prepared a heavenly city for them."

Hebrews 11:13, 16

Paul gives us a glimpse of the restoration to come in the physical universe:

"For all creation is waiting eagerly for that future day when God will reveal who his children really

> *are. Against its will, everything on earth was*
> *subjected to God's curse. All creation anticipates*
> *the day when it will join God's children in glorious*
> *freedom from death and decay. For we know that*
> *all creation has been groaning as in the pains of*
> *childbirth right up to the present time."*

Romans 8:19-22

When Adam and Eve sinned, God placed a curse on humanity, Satan, and nature. Death entered all of creation, and evil and suffering were allowed to bring destruction into God's world. But God revealed His plan of redemption before Adam and Eve left the Garden. The woman's offspring would defeat Satan and rescue all of God's creation from the curse (see Genesis 3:15). This "offspring" was Jesus, and He accomplished God's plan at the Cross.

What an amazing thought! Jesus' *physical* resurrection guaranteed the *physical* resurrection of His entire creation. Discovering this truth opened up a whole new set of questions for me. What will the new earth look like? Does the Bible describe it at all? Here are some things I found:

> *"Then I saw a new heaven and a new earth, for*
> *the old heaven and the old earth had disappeared.*
> *And the sea was also gone. And I saw the holy*
> *city, the new Jerusalem, coming down from God*
> *out of heaven like a beautiful bride prepared for*
> *her husband...So he (an angel) took me in spirit*
> *to a great, high mountain, and he showed me*
> *the holy city, Jerusalem, descending out of heaven*
> *from God. It was filled with the glory of God*
> *and sparkled like a precious gem, crystal clear like*
> *jasper. Its walls were broad and high, with twelve*

gates guarded by twelve angels…The angel who talked to me held in his hand a gold measuring stick to measure the city, its gates, and its wall. When he measured it, he found it was a square, as wide as it was long. In fact, it was in the form of a cube, for its length and width and height were each 1400 miles. Then he measured the walls and found them to be 216 feet thick (the angel used a standard human measure)."

Revelation 21:1-2, 10-12a, 15-17

I believe that although there is symbolic language in this description of the new Jerusalem, it's a real place. That's the reason for the concrete, "standard human measure" measuring by the angel. It was like saying, "Though you can't begin to describe it with human language, this beautiful, eternal city physically exists and will be redeemed humanity's perfect eternal home."

"No temple could be seen in the city, for the Lord God Almighty and the Lamb are its temple. And the city has no need of sun or moon, for the glory of God illuminates the city, and the Lamb is its light. The nations of the earth will walk in its light, and the rulers of the world will come and bring their glory to it. Its gates never close at the end of the day because there is no night. And all the nations will bring their glory and honor into the city. Nothing evil will be allowed to enter—no one who practices shameful idolatry and dishonesty—but only those whose names are written in the Lamb's Book of Life."

Revelation 21:22-27

"And the angel showed me a pure river with the water of life, clear as crystal, flowing from the throne of God and of the Lamb, coursing down the center of the main street. On each side of the river grew a tree of life, bearing twelve crops of fruit, with a fresh crop each month. The leaves were used for medicine to heal the nations. No longer will anything be cursed. For the throne of God and of the Lamb will be there, and his servants will worship him...And they will reign forever and ever."

Revelation 22:1-3, 5b

"In Jerusalem, the Lord Almighty will spread a wonderful feast for everyone around the world. It will be a delicious feast of good food, with clear, well-aged wine and choice beef. In that day he will remove the cloud of gloom, the shadow of death that hangs over the earth. He will swallow up death forever! The Sovereign Lord will wipe away all tears. He will remove forever all insults and mockery against his land and people. The Lord has spoken!

In that day the people will proclaim, 'This is our God. We trusted in him, and he saved us. This is the Lord, in whom we trusted. Let us rejoice in the salvation he brings!'"

Isaiah 25:6-9

Jesus also talked about the coming feast in His eternal Kingdom: *"And I tell you this, that many Gentiles will come from all over the world and sit down with Abraham, Isaac, and Jacob at the feast in the Kingdom of Heaven"* (Matthew 8:11).

What rich and detailed descriptions of a place we grow up believing is shadowy and lifeless! The Bible presents the new heavens and new earth as a real place with real people, doing real things, in real relationship with God and each other. If it were anything less, Satan would be a partial victor, and we know he's a defeated foe. I think that's why he likes to rob believers of any anticipation of our beautiful eternal home—in the end, it will be his only victory.

There's more, all throughout Scripture. Take some time to "explore" your eternal home and get to know what you can about it. You may be surprised just how much God has actually told us, not only about its physical nature, but also about the joys that await us. Many chapters in the second half of Isaiah describe the rescue, restoration and reunion of His children—all of which produce unending joy in His presence (see especially chapters 35, 49, 51, 54, 55, 60-62). What you discover will increase your desire for Christ; your anticipation of heaven will grow, motivating you to spend your life inviting others to know your King and become part of His Kingdom.

The Resurrection Body

> *"And even we Christians, although we have the Holy Spirit within us as a foretaste of future glory, also groan to be released from pain and suffering. We, too, wait anxiously for that day when God will give us our full rights as his children, including the new bodies he has promised us."*
>
> Romans 8:23

Jesus' death and resurrection weren't just to save the human soul, as if God decided to scrap everything else that sin's curse had ruined. That would be admitting defeat and cutting His losses. If the Bible presents a picture of our God at all, it certainly isn't that one. Throughout Scripture, God is Sovereign over all things: every nation and ruler, every circumstance and moment. And He's never defeated, by human or spiritual enemy. Any victory that is less than complete over Satan and the curse wouldn't be much of a victory.

God created humans as fully physical and fully spiritual beings. To let go of one of these aspects of our humanity would make us less than what He made us to be. How could our lives in God's eternal Kingdom be *greater* than they are here if we'll be *less* than we are here? Therefore, one of the victories the Bible promises us is the resurrection of our physical bodies on the last day—the day of Christ's return. As early as the days of Job (thought to be before Abraham's descendants moved to Egypt), God made this plan known. Job, in his grief, was comforted by this truth:

> *"But as for me, I know that my Redeemer lives, and that he will stand upon the earth at last. And after my body has decayed, yet in my body I will see God! I will see him for myself. Yes, I will see him with my own eyes. I am overwhelmed at the thought!"*

Job 19:25-26

Isaiah also prophesied it:

> *"Yet we have this assurance: Those who belong to God will live;*

Their bodies will rise again!
Those who sleep in the earth
Will rise up and sing for joy!
For God's light of life will fall like dew
On his people in the place of the dead!"

Isaiah 26:19

But what about the New Testament? Did Jesus preach the resurrection of the dead? In a conversation with Martha, Jesus very clearly told her, as she grieved her brother's death, *"Your brother will rise again."*

"Yes," Martha said, "when everyone else rises, on resurrection day."

Jesus told her, *"I am the resurrection and the life. Those who believe in me, even though they die like everyone else, will live again. They are given eternal life for believing in me and will never perish. Do you believe this, Martha?"* (See John 11:23-26.)

Devout Jews knew that their prophets had spoken of the resurrection of the body. It wasn't a highly developed teaching, however. So in this conversation, Jesus hinted at the coming resurrection and how it would be accomplished. First, He said that He *is* the resurrection and He *is* life. As the source of all life, Jesus would soon be raised from death back to life—resurrection life. Second, He invited people to receive resurrection to new life by believing in Him. We can experience the same kind of resurrection life that He did, in spirit now and in body at the last day.

But Jesus didn't just hint at this astounding truth. That day in Bethany, at the home of His dear friends, He *demonstrated* it in the midst of their grief. Because Mary, Martha and Lazarus trusted their Friend and Lord, Jesus enacted a picture of what all believers will one day receive: the resurrection of their bodies to incorruptible life. He did it by raising Lazarus from physical death to physical life.

Like so many temporary pictures of eternal truth throughout God's Word, Lazarus' raising was also temporary. Lazarus eventually died again. But Jesus showed us His power over death that day. He doesn't just *give* life, He *is* life—the very source of it. He gave us physical life limited to years here on earth. But He also offers spiritual and physical life that will last forever with Him. Lazarus will be raised again, and this time it won't be temporary.

The raising of Lazarus was a limited picture of Jesus' resurrection power. Jesus' own resurrection fully revealed the truth of what will one day happen to all believers. Paul says in 1 Corinthians 15:48: *"Every human being has an earthly body just like Adam's, but our heavenly bodies will be **just like Christ's**."* And in Philippians 3:20-21, he says:

> *"But we are citizens of heaven, where the Lord Jesus Christ lives. And we are eagerly waiting for him to return as our Savior. He will take these weak mortal bodies of ours and change them into glorious bodies **like his own**, using the same mighty power that he will use to conquer everything, everywhere."*

So, to learn about our future resurrection bodies, we need to look at what Scripture says about Christ's resurrection body.

Jesus' resurrection body is recognizable. All who saw Him knew it was Him, even if His identity was initially hidden. Mary Magdalene confused Him with a gardener as she grieved alone near the tomb, but the moment He spoke her name, she knew Him. The disciples walking to Emmaus were kept from recognizing Jesus for a short time. Perhaps this was so that Jesus could actually explain the Scriptures to them without being drowned out by their excitement over seeing Him alive. All other times Jesus appeared to His followers, they immediately recognized Him.

Jesus' resurrection body is the same body He was born with. There were scars in His hands, feet and side. Though it was now changed—glorified and incorruptible— it was connected to the body that died. Paul explains a bit of this mystery with a word picture:

> *"When you put a seed into the ground, it doesn't grow into a plant unless it dies first. And what you put in the ground is not the plant that will grow, but only a bare seed of wheat or whatever you are planting. Then God gives it the new body he wants it to have. A different plant grown from each kind of seed…It is the same way with the resurrection of the dead. Our earthly bodies are planted in the ground when we die, but they will be raised to live forever."*

1 Corinthians 15:36-38, 42

Paul was answering what he considered a foolish question: What kind of bodies will the dead have when they are raised? (See v. 35-36.) Skeptics of the day were asking this question to point out what they saw as the absurdity of life coming from death. But Paul saw it happening all the time in nature. It seemed obvious to him that our current bodies are the seeds of our future bodies. Our resurrection bodies will come from our dying bodies. And just like the plants that grow from seeds, our new bodies will be far greater and vastly different from our bodies now.

Jesus' resurrection body was physical. He could be touched. John 20:17 implies that Mary held tightly to Jesus when she first saw Him alive. This prompted Him to finally pull away so that He could meet with the others. He invited the disciples to touch Him and see that He was flesh and blood (Luke 24:39). He ate with the disciples on more than one occasion, once for the very purpose of proving that He was a physical being and not a ghost.

Jesus' resurrection body had new abilities and qualities. He disappeared from sight as He ate with the disciples from Emmaus, and He appeared inside a locked room where the disciples were gathered. His last day on earth, He rose into the air, disappearing into the clouds.

Jesus lives in heaven *in His physical body* even today. He ascended in His physical body, and He'll return at His Second Coming in His physical body.

So what does Christ's body tell us about our future bodies? A great deal. They will be physical, but they will never die. *"Our bodies now disappoint us, but when they are raised, they will be full of glory. They are weak now, but when they are raised, they will be full of power"* (1 Corinthians 15:43). They will be recognizable even though they have been vastly improved. In them, we will still participate in many of the same activities: physical contact with others, eating, walking and talking, to name a few. And they may also have some new capabilities and qualities; what those are, we can only speculate.

As wonderful as all of this is, the most important thing about our resurrection bodies is that they'll be home to our perfect, sinless natures. We'll finally be free from the sin nature we were born with, free to fully be that "new creation" Christ Jesus made us into when we believed. What an incredible thought, never to even want to sin again!

I must say that having a picture like this of our future resurrection body thrills me greatly. After all, the part of my daughter that allowed me to relate to her during her life on earth was her physical body. I could see her, hear her, and hug her all because she was a physical being. I watched her grow into a physically beautiful young lady, even as she grew spiritually beautiful. I loved and appreciated both. And I long for the day when I'll be able to do all of those things with her again, this time as perfect people. That, and nothing less, will be the complete restoration of our relationship.

Relationships in Heaven

With a better understanding of what the Bible says about our eternal home—the new heavens and new earth—and about our resurrection bodies and perfect natures, we can now look at what our relationships will be like there.

The first thing we need to understand is that God *is* relationship. He didn't just create relationship; He is most fully expressed in it. The Bible teaches that God is Three in One—Father, Son, and Holy Spirit. God is love, and His love has been expressed in relationship from eternity past, long before He ever created man.

Because God is love and expresses Himself in relationship, He created us "in His image" for love and relationship. Our most important relationship is with Him; our next is with others. Jesus made this clear:

> *"And you must love the Lord your God with all your heart, all your soul, all your mind, and all your strength. The second is equally important: 'Love your neighbor as yourself.' No other commandment is greater than these."*

Mark 12:30-31

We see the beginning of man's relationships in the Garden. God created man and fellowshipped with him. They walked together and named all the animals together. God commissioned him to care for the earth, showing him all the provisions of the Garden. Then God gave him the restriction of that one tree. But God saw one thing in His good creation that was not good: *"It is not good for the man to be alone. I will make a companion who will help him"* (Genesis 2:18). Adam was not completely alone, in that he had relationship with God and caretaking interaction with the animals. But God knew Adam's love for Him would only be fully expressed as Adam loved another human being. The apostle John explained this when he wrote:

> *"Dear friends, since God loved us that much, we surely ought to love each other. No one has ever seen God. But if we love each other, God lives in us, and **his love has been brought to full expression through us.**"*

1 John 4:11-12

He said it even more forcefully like this:

> *"If someone says, 'I love God,' but hates a Christian brother or sister, that person is a liar; for if we don't love people we can see, how can we love God,*

74

whom we have not seen? And God himself has commanded that we must love not only him but our Christian brothers and sisters, too."

1 John 4:20-21

In God's eyes, our love for others is the completion of our love for Him. He doesn't see our healthy relationships with others as a threat to our relationship with Him, and neither should we. There certainly are relationships that become idolatrous, in which people put other people in place of God in their lives. But the godly relationships that God calls us to only help to express our love for Him more fully. They never diminish or take the place of our relationship with Him.

Yet there are some who teach that in heaven, we will (or should) desire only to be with God. Loving anyone else seems to them to be idolatrous and self-seeking. But, as Scripture says, God gives us relationships as an extension of His love for us and of our love for Him. It pleases Him when we enjoy His good gifts. Any good parent understands the joy of seeing his child delighting in his gifts given in love. Enjoying relationships with each other in heaven will be one way of loving our God who gave them to us, just as enjoying each other on this Earth expresses our love for God now.

Several months after the accident, the Holy Spirit showed me, as I studied a story in Luke 7, how much God values our relationships. It's the story of Jesus stopping a funeral procession, bringing a widow's son back to life, and giving him back to her.

7/15/2008

I confess that I didn't want to read this. I didn't want to hear about a mother who received her child back from the dead. Jesus, speak to me.

"When the Lord saw her, His heart overflowed with compassion. 'Don't cry!' He said" (v.13). Does Your heart overflow with compassion for me Lord? I've felt it, felt You. But each day, I need more. I'm like a sponge that soaks You in, but keeps getting wrung out by the sorrow of each day. Is this miracle a picture of something greater? Is it more than just a physical restoration of life? More than just an earthly relationship renewed? Lord, You came to bring eternal healing, eternal life. You gave the promise of physical resurrection and the restoration of all we've lost here in a fallen world.

I see here a picture of what Jesus has already done for Lauren spiritually, for she is alive. But I also see the promise of what He bought for us at the cross—physical resurrection, and restoration of interrupted or broken relationships. "And Jesus gave him back to his mother" (v. 15b).

If Jesus came only for this life, then this mother and son would still face final separation at death. Everyone Jesus raised from the dead while He was here eventually died again. But His sacrifice was too great for such a small outcome. Jesus conquered death completely. He purchased the full restoration of His entire creation.

So when I read this account and asked, "Why didn't You give Lauren back to me?" Jesus whispered, "I will give her back to you. I raised her up to real life that day, and I will one day give her back to you forever."

Jesus, help me to keep my eyes, heart and mind focused upon You. You purchased huge and mighty promises for Your children. Your suffering and death brought us so much more than life here on earth. The life You give is too big to be contained in or confined to this world. Thank You for making me a mother, and for understanding the greatest desire of a mother's heart. Thank You for fulfilling it forever.

In this account, the Holy Spirit began to show me one of the greatest purposes of the Cross—reconciliation. First and foremost with God:

"For since we were restored to friendship with God by the death of his Son while we were still his enemies, we will certainly be delivered from eternal punishment by his life. So now we can rejoice in our wonderful new relationship with God—all because of what our Lord Jesus Christ has done for us in making us friends of God."

Romans 5:10-11

Jesus made it very clear that reconciliation was to extend to our relationships with people as well:

"So if you are standing before the altar in the Temple, offering a sacrifice to God, and you

> *suddenly remember that someone has something against you, leave your sacrifice there beside the altar. Go and be reconciled to that person. Then come and offer your sacrifice to God."*

Matthew 5:23-24

Because Adam and Eve sinned in the Garden, breaking their relationship with God, God's eternal plan was to reconcile man to Himself. He did it at the Cross. This reconciliation with God must lead us also to reconcile with others, for we can only be most fully who we're meant to be when we're in relationship.

Now, looking ahead to the new heavens and the new earth, if we're to be made complete there, then it must be in the context of relationships. I believe this means two things: 1) the relationships we had on earth with believers will continue and grow even deeper, and 2) our relationships on earth are pictures of greater relationships we'll one day have.

First, let's look at the continuing nature of our relationships with others in heaven. Because we'll be fully ourselves, aware and remembering, our earthly relationships will be a big part of our lives in eternity. Otherwise, we would be less in heaven than we were on earth; a big part of us would be gone. If our relationships will be over, that would mean they had no real meaning or purpose on earth. We know because of God's nature, however, that they're of paramount importance. So they won't be over. I'll still be my parents' daughter and my children's mother. Since we're first and foremost God's children, they'll also be my brothers and sisters in Christ. I'll enjoy equal and deeply intimate relationships with them and with so many others because I'll be unhindered by sin.

That brings up the question of broken relationships between brothers and sisters in Christ. Many of us have trouble understanding what they'll be like in heaven. We may or may not have forgiven and received forgiveness in troubled and broken relationships. Some have been restored. But some relationships are no longer close and may never be restored on earth. Will we just avoid these people for eternity? Will we forget past hurts and injustices and trust fully again without ever working things out? I don't think so, because our God is a God of justice, and He never just looks the other way where sin and brokenness are concerned. He's the God of reconciliation. I believe He will preside over the restoration of our estranged relationships, bringing everything to light and revealing the truth of all that happened. Then He'll give us a new beginning based on our perfected ability to trust and be trustworthy.

Now, let's look at the way so many of our relationships here on earth point to greater realities of relationship in heaven. Relationships with parents point to our relationship with God, our Father. Parenting our children reveals a great deal about our Father's heart toward us as His children. Whether we've had good relationships with our parents and/or children or not, in heaven, our greatest desire for a trusting, secure relationship with a parent will be beautifully fulfilled with God the Father.

Other family relationships point us to our eternal family, the family of God. This may be a clichéd expression, but it was a firm teaching of Jesus. When He was told that His mother and brothers were looking for Him, Jesus replied, *"My mother and my brothers are all those who hear the message of God and obey it"* (Luke 8:21). By saying this, He didn't disown His family, He expanded it. Our brothers and sisters in Christ around the world truly are our family. It will be even more so in heaven. We'll have an incredible family, made up of everyone who loves Christ, from Abraham to the last person who arrives. And we'll have all eternity to get to know each other.

Marriage is probably the most beautiful relationship picture we have here on earth. But there is great misunderstanding concerning its continuity, or lack of it, in heaven. This most likely comes from a passage of Scripture in which the Sadducees presented Jesus with a convoluted story about the widow of seven brothers (each who died while married to her). The Sadducees then asked which brother would be married to her in heaven. They didn't want an answer, they were merely trying stump Jesus and prove that a coming resurrection wasn't logical or possible. Jesus answered them like this: *"Marriage is for people here on earth. But that is not the way it will be in the age to come. For those worthy of being raised from the dead won't be married then"* (Luke 20:34-35). Because of this answer, many people think their marriage relationships will end in heaven. Randy Alcorn, however, in his book *Heaven*, does an exceptional job of making the greater reality of marriage in heaven beautifully clear:

> "The Bible does *not* teach there will be no marriage in Heaven. In fact, it makes clear there *will* be marriage in Heaven. What it says is that there will be *one* marriage, between Christ and his bride—and we'll all be part of it. Paul links human marriage to the higher reality it mirrors: 'For this reason a man will leave his father and

mother and be united to his wife, and the two will become one flesh. This is a profound mystery—but I am talking about Christ and the church' (Ephesians 5:31-32).

"The one-flesh marital union we know on Earth is a signpost pointing to our relationship with Christ as our bridegroom. Once we reach the destination, the signpost becomes unnecessary. That one marriage—our marriage to Christ—will be so completely satisfying that even the most wonderful earthly marriage couldn't be as fulfilling.

"Earthly marriage is a shadow, a copy, an echo of the true and ultimate marriage. Once that ultimate marriage begins, at the Lamb's wedding feast, all the human marriages that pointed to it will have served their noble purpose and will be assimilated into the one great marriage they foreshadowed."[8]

So, does that mean our earthly marriage relationships will just fall to the wayside? Will it be the end of closeness to our spouses? Again, from Randy Alcorn:

"My wife, Nanci, is my best friend and my closest sister in Christ. Will we become more distant in the new world? Of course not—we'll become closer, I'm convinced. The God who said "It is not good for the man to be alone" (Genesis 2:18) is the giver and blesser of our relationship. Life

---

[8]   Randy Alcorn, *Heaven* (Carol Stream, IL: Tyndale House Publishers, Inc., 2004), 350.

on this earth matters. What we do here touches strings that reverberate for all eternity. Nothing will take away from the fact that Nanci and I are marriage partners here and that we invest so much of our lives in each other, serving Christ together. I fully expect no one besides God will understand me better on the New Earth, and there's nobody whose company I'll seek and enjoy more than Nanci's."[9]

Alcorn points out that Jesus said the *institution* of earthly marriage will end as our marriage to Him begins, but He never even hinted that deep relationships between married people will end. Alcorn then gives an illustration of the way our marriage relationships will change but still exist. He likens it to the way different partnerships on earth can change; tennis, business, or pinochle partnerships often end, but carry over into permanent friendships. "I expect that to be true on the New Earth for family members and friends who stood by each other here."[10]

Continuation of relationships in the new heavens and new earth is one of the greatest comforts offered to followers of Christ. Because of it, we don't have to *"be full of sorrow like people who have no hope"* (1 Thessalonians 4:13). Instead,

> "We on this dying Earth can relax and rejoice for our loved ones who are in the presence of Christ...Our parting is not the end of our relationship, only an interruption. We have not 'lost' them, because we know where they are. They are experiencing the joy of Christ's

---

9   Alcorn, 350-351.
10   Alcorn, 351.

presence in a place so wonderful that Christ called it Paradise. And one day, we're told, in a magnificent reunion, they and we will be with the Lord forever. Therefore encourage each other with these words' (1 Thessalonians 4:17-18)."[11]

---

[11]   Alcorn, 73.

Chapter 5—How to Go On?

The Circle
6/12/08

Lost, displaced, misplaced, longing for another place.
Disconnected, disinterested, dispassionate,
Aimless, purposeless, drifting away.
Am I depressed? I don't know…
What can I do? What is the answer?
I feel trapped here, in a place I don't belong
And I don't want to be.
What now? Where do I go from here?
In some ways, things are just now becoming real.
At a time when people seem to think I'm healing,
I'm just now beginning to hurt.
The pain is unrelenting,
I wake everyday to the same thing…
She's not here.
I know I have not lost her,
I have just lost contact with her,
For now.

It's that now that seems endless, unrelenting, unbending.
It weighs on me more and more.
I feel like I will never escape it.
But I will.
And so I focus on what is to come,
And find comfort there.
Only, that puts me right back up at the top...
Lost, displaced, misplaced, longing for another place.

Apathy

I'm so very grateful to the Holy Spirit for leading me to the truth about the hope we have in Christ. For all who put their faith in Christ, God's Word guarantees life after death in His presence, resurrection on the last day, and a beautiful eternal home. Without this hope, I would either be dead or crazy, and I'm only partially joking when I say that. If the reality I live in now were the only reality there is, I'm not sure I would've been able to survive that first year of grief. Even today, I wonder if I would ever be able to rejoin life here and find joy in it again without the promises of God. I want to say I would've made it, because I have a wonderful husband and two amazing sons who fill my life with love and laughter. But I don't know. Let's just say I'm thankful I won't ever have to find out.

Though I understood the truth of Lauren's life now and the promise of my reunion with her one day, I wasn't living it. But I wanted to. The greater reality of eternity had to start affecting my life in this world.

Instead, my understanding created a new struggle. I didn't want to stay in this world, much less be connected and involved with it. All I wanted to do was go to be with Lauren where all the pain would end. I wasn't suicidal, because I didn't want to die; I just wanted to live somewhere else. I had no desire to be here. I didn't want to live in the present because my daughter was no longer in it. She was in my past, and she's in my future. The present was too hard.

Learning about God's promises of life in the new heavens and new earth made me very apathetic about this life. In light of the life to come, this present life had dulled to an awful gray. The only color left in it was Scott, Jordan and Jonathan. On June 30th, 2008, I wrote in my journal: *"The promises of heaven and reunion are wonderful, but they don't erase the emptiness of now."* A few days earlier I'd written a lengthy entry about the apathy I was slogging through. I want to share it here almost in its entirety because I struggled with apathy for many months. Even after the worst had passed, the feeling still came and went for two more years. I wrote about it several times, but this one entry will give a good picture of how I felt, and how the Holy Spirit counseled me through God's Word.

6/24/2008

> *I'm experiencing a greater and greater detachment from this life and a growing desire to give up. I'm so weary, so tired of being here! And God is faithfully meeting me in this weakness. Some scriptures:*

> *"We are pressed on every side by troubles, but we are <u>not</u> crushed and broken. We are perplexed, but we do <u>not</u> give up and quit. We are hunted down, but God <u>never</u> abandons us. We get knocked down, but we get up again and keep going. Through suffering, these bodies of ours constantly share in*

the death of Jesus so that the life of Jesus may also be seen in our bodies."

2 Corinthians 4:8-10

"My health may fail, and my spirit may grow weak, but God remains the strength of my heart; He is mine forever."

Psalm 73:26

"May the Lord bring you into an ever deeper understanding of the love of God and the endurance that comes from Christ."

2 Thessalonians 3:5

"Those who live to please the Spirit will harvest everlasting life from the Spirit. So don't get tired of doing what is good. Don't get discouraged and give up, for we will reap a harvest of blessing at the appropriate time."

Galatians 6:8b-9

"Think about all He (Jesus) endured when sinful people did such terrible things to Him, so that you don't become weary and give up."

Hebrews 12:3

The Lord is saying to me that my strength, endurance, and ability not to give up come only and always from Him.

God never abandons me.
God remains the strength of my heart.
Endurance comes from Christ.

I will harvest everlasting life from the Spirit if I don't get tired or discouraged, or give up.

Think about all Jesus endured...so that I don't get tired and give up.

I'm at a point in my journey through grief where I'm very tired of this life. I feel trapped here, and I want to go Home. It's all I can do to endure just one day at a time. My spirit grows weak, and my health fails, so I just want to give up. But God promises that He's the strength of my heart, He's my endurance. I may never find happiness in this life again. Right now I don't want to find it. All I want is to be done here. But only God determines that; so while I remain, the answer to not giving up is Him. My strength is Him, my encouragement and example is His endurance through His own suffering. My motivation is the joy set before me.

"For our present troubles are quite small and won't last very long. Yet they produce for us an immeasurably great glory that will last forever. So we don't look at the troubles we can see right now, rather we look forward to what we have not yet seen. For the troubles we see will soon be over, but the joys to come will last forever."

2 Corinthians 4:17-18

> *"There is life after death! Knowing that we will live forever with God in a place without sin and suffering can help us <u>live above the pain</u> that we face in this life." (Life Application Bible Notes)*[12]

Over the course of many "sessions" with the Holy Spirit, He dealt with the apathy that threatened to derail me. The truth of His presence with me and the eternal promises from His Word began to help me "live above the pain" of my grief. But it was a battle, a battle for what I called the "Land of His Promises." It was a land I wanted desperately to live in.

I couldn't live in the past; I didn't want to live in the present, so the only place I wanted to be was in the future. But since my future is in God's hands alone, I had to learn to live in the present with His promises to carry me through and even above the pain of grief. I had to let the future affect the present. This was easier said than done. But nothing is impossible with God.

Relating to Others

Before I continue my battle with apathy, I want to talk about a couple of other things that made getting on with life such a struggle for me. They fed my desire to withdraw.

I learned very early in the grieving process that there were people in my life I thought of as "safe people." They were the ones that came and just sat with me, or cried with me, or let me talk about the same things over and over. They didn't try to fix me, comfort me, or want me to be

---

[12] *Life Application Study Bible,* Notes and Bible Helps (Wheaton, IL: Tyndale House Publishers, Inc., 1988, 1989, 1990, 1991, 1993, 1996), 1839.

better. They didn't ask me how I was, because they knew I had no acceptable answer. They just told me how sorry they were and hurt with me. They let me be a mess. They let me hide.

But I couldn't stay hidden. Life went on. We were involved in the worship ministry of our church, and each week I would stand on stage and sing worship songs and cry. I knew I didn't have to be strong in my grief. I could be real, because our church has a heart for the broken. But people looked to us as strong leaders in faith. I didn't want them to think it was faltering (even though it was under heavy attack) or that God couldn't carry us through this. At the same time, I wasn't about to pretend I was over my grief. That would be like saying Lauren wasn't very important to me.

Then there were my friends whose children were growing up with ours. I couldn't hide from them either. Jonathan, our youngest son, was a seventh-grader in the youth group, so many of my friendships revolved around what the kids were doing. It suddenly became very hard to maintain them, because every time I was with these friends, I felt like I was missing an arm and everyone was trying very hard not to look. Inside, I was screaming, *"You have all of your children and I don't!"* But no one seemed to notice.

I'm sure they knew I was hurting; it's just that they had no idea what to say or do about it. I never used to know either. As time passed, they went on with their lives—with all of their children. Because I still had Jordan and Jonathan here, I could be a real part of most conversations. But then someone would talk about the upcoming prom and shopping for dresses and who her daughter's date was going to be. Disconnect. I could no longer participate in that conversation, and it hurt. It wasn't their fault, I just didn't know how to handle those things I was no longer part of because of Lauren's absence.

There were a *lot* of normal conversations that I couldn't handle anymore. One mom would say to another mom, "I heard your daughter almost had an accident the other day." And that mom would reply, "Yes, it was so frightening, but God was good and no one was hurt." What was I supposed to say to that? "Well, I guess God wasn't good to us, because our daughter died?" So I would say nothing, but the screaming in my head would begin: *How can you talk about this in front of me? Does no one remember that my child is gone and I am dying inside?*

As real as I could be with God and with my "safe people," I found that I often put on a false front with others, while the real me was a total mess inside.

6/30/2008

> *I'm struggling with how to relate to others right now, to those friends I love but who aren't one of the few close to me.*
>
> *Do they really want to know how I am or would it make them uncomfortable if I were honest with them?*
>
> *Do I want them to mention my grief or not?*
>
> *Do I want them to talk about their lives with their daughters or stop talking about them around me?*
>
> *Which ones are okay when I talk about my pain and struggle and which ones aren't?*

My friends and so many others who watched our family had no way to understand what we were going through. Most people were sensitive enough to realize that. But while

I know that it's important never to tell someone that you know what they're going through unless you've been through it yourself, I've learned that "I can't begin to understand what you're going through" is one of the most isolating statements anyone can make.

What I felt most in a group of friends was ALONE. I was the only mom in my circle of friends, and even acquaintances, who was missing a child. And I knew, because of that, people struggled to relate to me, and I to them. But they watched me.

6/30/2008

There are those who want to see my journey of faith through tragedy as a straight line to God. They want to see a faith that has never wavered, a heart that isn't too wounded to heal, a spiritual giant that can be a comfort to them by never doubting God. I pray that I can be that kind of example, a light for the goodness and faithfulness of God. He has been good and faithful.

But my journey hasn't been a straight line so far. My faith has faltered, I've stumbled, I'm not whole. The pain has overwhelmed me and still does. The promises of heaven and reunion are wonderful, but they don't erase the emptiness of now.

I love the Lord Jesus with all my heart, but my grief is still messy. I'm often confused; I'm still not sure I won't drown. I feel these things simultaneously with the assurance that God will carry me through this and I won't be destroyed by it.

So often I find what's going on inside of me much too complicated to put into words for others. Grief over the loss of a child is so very complicated! I had no way of knowing that before, so how can I expect anyone who hasn't experienced it to understand? Much less really want to hear it?

We like our spiritual lessons to come neatly wrapped with a bow on top. We like our human examples and pictures of truth to be clear and tidy, unencumbered by weakness and failure. It makes us feel better about God. We can put Him in a little box where He doesn't feel as untamed, as uncontrolled by us. If we can watch someone go through our worst nightmare and come out strong and unscathed, then it makes us feel a bit less vulnerable and God a little more predictable.

But reality is never that neat. And the reality of grief is, in a word, messy. I never knew that until now. The magnitude of its messiness is hard to deal with. So how can I expect others to?

The way Jesus handled grief is, of course, most amazing and real. It captures and meets head-on, all of the messiness. When Jesus raised Lazarus from the dead, He fully dismissed the power of death over His children, while at the same time acknowledging the enormity of the pain it causes. On one hand, He reassures those grieving that He has conquered death and is eternal life. On the other, He enters their grief, experiencing fully the depth of pain and loss death brings.

Oh, that we could learn from His example, that we'd learn to comfort, encourage, and reassure believers with God's promises while still acknowledging the enormity of loss death brings in this life.

If I've learned anything about grief, it's that everyone goes through it differently. The "stages" of grief are never linear or orderly. My own experience didn't give me easy answers for others going through their own tragedy. But it did make me more willing to reach out to them. I learned to be sensitive to people and their unique situations, listening more than talking and taking my cues from them. Now I pray for wisdom to minister to others as Jesus did, entering their hurt through shared experience and lifting their eyes to the promises of eternity.

People don't have to experience grief or tragedy to reach out to grieving friends. It does take, however, asking God for the courage, wisdom and sensitivity, to meet them wherever they are. They need friends who will give them room to express their pain without wanting to make it go away. It hurts to see others in pain, but mourners must go *through* the sorrow to get to the other side. Being a "safe person" who's willing to hurt with them gives them permission not to be alright. One day they will be, but it will happen in their own time.

For those mourning one who's died in the Lord, they need to be pointed often to the promise of heaven. They need to be reminded of the new life their loved one now lives, and of the joyous anticipation of a coming reunion. Friends who understood and encouraged me with these truths were my greatest comfort. My joy in this life now comes from two promises: 1) that Christ will never leave me, and 2) that I'll spend eternity with Lauren and all of my loved ones in His presence. *"For to me, to live is Christ and to die is gain"* (Philippians 1:21).

The Spotlight

There's a story in Acts 14 about Paul and Barnabas being worshiped as gods after they healed a crippled man in Lystra.

> *"But when Paul and Barnabas heard what was happening, they tore their clothing in dismay and ran out among the people, shouting, 'Friends, why are you doing this? We are merely human beings like yourselves! We have come to bring you the Good News..."*

v. 14-15a

Paul and Barnabas knew it was God's power, not their own, that healed the man. They didn't deserve any more credit for it than I do.

And that's the point the Holy Spirit made to me when I read the story. God was at work in my life in a very public way. In the early months of my grief, I had no idea people were watching. I was too numb, the confusion too loud. So it always shocked me when someone would come up and take my hand to tell me how strong I was, what an inspiration I was to them. I wasn't strong, I was about to fly into a million pieces. My silent prayers when I was out in public were often, "Lord, please hold me together!"

And so I would stare and say something like, "Anything strong you see is God, not me. He's holding the pieces of me in His hands." It wasn't possible then for me to take credit for anything good or strong that people saw in my life.

But the Holy Spirit still warned me with that story.

4/3/2008

As time goes on and God faithfully carries me and empowers me, there will continue to be opportunities to receive the praises of men. Satan will attempt to deceive me with my own pride. I don't want to fall into his trap. I want to point to God <u>every time</u> people try to give me praise. I truly am nothing on my own, and anything they see in my life worthy of praise cannot be me because I'm too broken.

Eventually, I did become more aware that people were watching our entire family. I didn't want to fake it, but I also didn't want to dishonor God. I didn't have to be strong to honor Him; I just had to give Him the credit for His faithfulness.

6/23/2008

"Don't you remember that our ancestor Abraham was declared right with God because of what he did when he offered his son Isaac on the altar? You see, he was trusting God so much that he was willing to do whatever God told him to do. His faith was made complete by what he did—by his actions."

James 2:21-22

People are watching me closely to see if my love for Jesus and faith in Him are real or if they'll crumble. The only way for them to see it is through my actions…Now that my life's in the spotlight and people are watching me, I'll prove <u>something</u> to them with my life, my actions. I'll show them

> *one of two things: 1) my faith wasn't real, sending*
> *the false message that God isn't real or isn't really*
> *trustworthy, OR, 2) God <u>is</u> real, and worthy of*
> *my trust, obedience, and love, even when I don't*
> *understand His ways. Will I obey even when I*
> *don't understand what He's doing? Or will I reject*
> *God's way because I don't trust Him or like the*
> *way He's asking me to go?*

The confusing part of these questions was whether to answer them with my heart or with my head. My head knew that everything I believed was true, but my heart now lagged far behind. God's goodness and faithfulness had always felt good before, and now they didn't. I wanted to proclaim the truth with my life and have it *feel* true, and it didn't always.

But when I looked at Abraham climbing that mountain with his son and fire and wood and no animal to sacrifice, I knew he didn't feel good either. I could feel every weighted step, the stoop in his shoulders, and the knot in his chest. And still he trudged on in obedience to the God he trusted more than he loved his son. His God was good, and faithful, and would bring Isaac back to life if that's what it took. Because God made Abraham a promise, and Isaac was the beginning of its fulfillment.

God has made all of His children a promise—that they'll live forever with Him. And no matter how untrue that felt to me when Lauren died, I refused to stop believing it. Or living it. But sometimes it got tiring.

7/11/2008

Luke 6:6-16. Jesus heals a man with a withered
hand on the Sabbath.

As I read the account of this man's healing, for the first time I felt the glare of the spotlight he must have felt as Jesus called to him. "Come and stand here where everyone can see." So the man came forward. Why did Jesus put him on display?

Jesus' ministry was public, bold, and for everyone. He understood that people needed to see the reality of God's life-changing power. Today, people need the same thing. Is the gospel real in its power to change and save lives, or is it powerless in life?

In some ways I've felt like a spectacle over the last five months. I feel like people are watching for me to be healed. I've resented being in the spotlight, and I've run from it. I just want to blend in and not be the focus of people's scrutiny. But the message I've received all week from the Holy Spirit is that God wants me in the spotlight so that He can reveal His power to those watching. And if I realize He's in the spotlight with me and His purpose is for good, not harm, for saving my life, not destroying it, then I can rest under His wings. He will proclaim the message and He will judge the responses of others. It's not my job to convince anyone of the truth, and it's not my job to heal myself. These are the Lord's jobs from start to finish. All that Jesus asks me to do is to step into the spotlight, let Him make the truth visible to all, and trust Him to heal me. If I'm willing to do this, many will have the opportunity to see God at work in a real life.

Am I willing to do my part, to remain visible? I felt all alone in the spotlight. But God revealed

> *to me through this account that I'm not alone here. He has me here for incredible good, not for harm, both for me and for all who can see what He's doing.*

I mulled over this lesson for a day or two, wondering if the man with the deformed hand was as reluctant to be in the spotlight as I was. Was it as hard for him to be watched and scrutinized by the crowd as it was for me? And then I realized that *Jesus* was the one in the spotlight. He was the one the people and religious leaders watched. He just called the man to join Him there. I believe the man saw the love, forgiveness, and desire to heal in Jesus' eyes, and so he came. He trusted and he came.

7/12/2008

> *Jesus You have called to me…I feel deformed like an amputee. I don't want attention drawn to myself. I stopped trusting you. I stopped seeing Your face of love, and hearing Your voice of mercy. I wanted to come to You in faith, but I couldn't. I felt all alone in the spotlight. Thank you for showing me that You've been here all the time. It's always been Your spotlight. You just brought me into it with You. Just like the people were intently watching and scrutinizing You then, so people today are watching You in me to see if You're really who You say You are. They need to see if You really deliver on Your promises. I confess that I doubted You, and for that my heart breaks with sorrow. Please forgive me for ever doubting Your love, power, and faithfulness.*

You've called me into the spotlight so You can do mighty things, and in faith I will come. Please don't ever let me think that the spotlight is for me. I'm just the object lesson, here because I'm with You. And yet, I know You love me beyond all I can imagine. I know I'm safe here with You. I don't ever want to leave Your side again, no matter where You take me. I love You so much.

The next day, the Holy Spirit showed me another lesson about the spotlight. As I've said, I felt very uncomfortable in it. Part of that was because I felt alone and on display; God showed me that wasn't true. But the other reason I felt so uncomfortable is because I didn't know how to act. And that was because my heart and my head were not in agreement with each other. My head knew every promise of hope God had given me backward and forward. My heart was having trouble holding on to those promises. My head said that Jesus has made death powerless over the believer, so my loss is no big deal. My heart said the separation of death is so devastating, I may never recover.

I would have inner conversations that went something like this: *Should I act like I'm doing well, or like I really feel? If I act too normal, they might think I'm okay, and I'm not. But if I'm full of sorrow with no hope, I'll dishonor God. Maybe I'll try to be at peace yet sad, so that God will be honored while my pain is still visible. After all, I don't want people to think I'm over this, because I'll never be, but I don't want people treating me like I'll never see Lauren again because I will...* Wow. I was a mess.

But as I reread my journal entry from 7/11, I saw something in my own words: *"He will proclaim the message and He will judge the responses of others."*

I wrote those words without understanding what God was trying to tell me. But as I read them again, He opened my heart to their meaning: Because people watch me so closely now, I feel awkward and on display, like I have to act a certain way or convey a certain message. And I judge their responses to me too: "they might think...," I don't want people to think..." But, I don't have to figure out what message to give others, what truth about God to portray. Jesus, through the Holy Spirit in me, will make the message loud and clear, whatever it might be for each encounter. And I mustn't judge what others say and do around me. Only Jesus can judge people's true responses to His message given through my life.

Lord Jesus, thank You so much for showing me these things—the sins of not trusting You, of self-effort, and of judging others. Please forgive me, cleanse me, and free me. Fill me, Jesus, with your amazing Spirit. Help me trust You to live, speak, and respond through me. I want to rest under Your wings, open my heart completely, and let You share with others the message You have for them in me.

It wasn't always easy, but I did learn to rest in the spotlight that belonged to Jesus, not to me. He gave me opportunities to share much of what I was learning about heaven and our eternal future. And people listened. In fact, the Holy Spirit showed me that Lauren's home-going and our search for God's promises have done much to lift many eyes and hearts to the wonders of the life to come. He confirmed it with this story:

> "When a shepherd seeks to lead his sheep to better grass up the winding, thorny mountain paths, he often finds that the sheep will not follow him. They fear the unknown ridges and the sharp rocks. The shepherd will then reach into the flock and take a little lamb on one arm and another on his other arm. Then he starts up the precipitous pathway. Soon the two mother sheep begin to follow, and afterward the entire flock. Thus, they ascend the tortuous path to greener pastures.
>
> "So it is with the Good Shepherd. Sometimes He reaches into the flock and takes a lamb to Himself. He uses the experience to lead His people, to lift them to new heights of commitment as they follow the little lamb all the way home."[13]

God indeed lifted our eyes when He carried Lauren home. He rekindled, and even created in many for the first time, the anticipation we are called to for heaven and Christ's return:

> *"And now the prize awaits me—the crown of righteousness that the Lord, the righteous Judge, will give me on that great day of his return. And*

---

[13] Erwin W. Lutzer, *One Minute After You Die* (Chicago: Moody Press, 1997), 75.

> the prize is not just for me but for **all who eagerly
> look forward to his glorious return.**"

2 Timothy 4:8

Until that day, we are called to live in the spotlight:

> *"But this precious treasure—this light and power
> that now shines within us—is held in perishable
> containers, that is, in our weak bodies. So everyone
> can see that our glorious power is from God and
> is not our own."*

2 Corinthians 4:7

Pink Pearls

The lessons of the spotlight were one step of my journey out of apathy toward reconnecting with this life. Another would involve a battle to fully occupy the Land of God's Promises. I couldn't keep standing on its border, unable to go in. But I was clinging to things that held me back.

During the summer of 2008, I decided to go to youth camp as a cook. Lauren's friends had become such a blessing to me as we grieved together that I was really looking forward to spending a few days just loving on them. Both my boys were there too; Jonathan as a camper, and Jordan as the videographer. I had a wonderful time, until the last night.

Exhaustion, not enough time alone with God, and watching camp go on without Lauren, all worked together to send me into a tailspin on Thursday evening before the service. I ended up in a room behind the kitchen, sobbing and blubbering about why was I at camp instead of her, and about my fear that I would forget my daughter's voice and the feel of her hair. I felt like I was leaving her behind.

My fellow cooks, all close friends, tried to comfort me. But I couldn't pull myself together. So after everyone left for the service, I slowly made my way down to the open-air tabernacle. Because I was still in melt-down mode, I stayed out among the trees nearby. I could hear the worship music. I looked into the sky and found myself telling God that I needed to feel His arms around me right then, not through someone else, but *His* arms. After a few moments, I went to the edge of the tabernacle and sat on the short wall at the back to listen. The speaker was beginning his message. I almost dared God to speak to me.

Near the end of his talk, Zane told the story of a little girl who saved up her money and bought a plastic pink pearl necklace. It was her most treasured possession, because when she wore it, she felt like a princess. So she wore it all the time, even to bed.

One night, her daddy came to her room as usual to tuck her into bed. Only this time he asked her a question. "Honey, do you love daddy?"

"Oh yes!" she replied. "Of course I do!"

"Do you trust me enough to give me your plastic pink pearl necklace?"

The little girl's face fell as her hand instinctively covered the pearls. "Oh, Daddy! I love you so much, but I can't give you my pearls."

Daddy quickly reassured her, "It's ok, sweetheart. I know you love me. Don't worry about the pearls." He kissed her forehead tenderly, turned out the light, and left the room.

For the next several nights, the little girl's father asked her the same question, and each night her answer was the same. Until one night, when he came into the room to find her sitting on the edge of her bed. Tears were streaming down her face as she held something tightly in her hands.

"Honey, what's wrong?" Daddy asked her gently, brushing the tears from her cheeks.

"Daddy," she choked, "I really do love you very much, and I want to give you my pink pearls." She opened her fisted hands to reveal the strand.

The little girl's father smiled just a bit and slowly took the plastic pink pearl necklace. Then he reached into his back pocket and pulled out a real pink pearl necklace, fastening it around her neck.

From the first sentence of this story, I recognized it, because I had told it many times myself. It's a story that illustrates how we cling to the worthless treasures of this world, the ones we can work for ourselves. But God wants us to trust Him enough to let go of them so that He can give us true, eternal treasures, the ones we can't afford. The ones that Jesus bought to give us as a gift. The only difference in Zane's version of the story was that the pearls were pink. I wondered at the time why they were. I had never even seen pink pearls.

As Zane finished the story, he asked the kids to think and pray about the "treasures" God wanted them to surrender to Him. I knew the Holy Spirit was calling me to do the same. But I was emotionally wrung out, and truthfully, I didn't want to surrender anything that night. So I loved on my boys and went to bed.

The next morning, I got my journal and began to write.

7/18/2008, AM

What is it that God is asking me to give Him? What thing am I holding onto? Is it my relationship with Lauren? Is it my "right" to have life turn out the way I want it to? What, Lord? What are my "plastic pearls"?

I worked through what the Holy Spirit was showing me and saw that I was trying to hold on to the past—I wanted my daughter back. I was also holding on to the future I wanted with her—her college years, marriage, children, and being her confidante through it all. It was taken from me, but I had not surrendered it.

I haven't acknowledged that God has the right to decide the path of her life and mine. I'm holding onto a future earthly dream of our relationship, even though I can never have that. And I'm angry that God took it away. I'm not okay with it.

I think God is telling me to really work through who Lauren belongs to. God created her, and gave her to me, even as she still belonged to Him. He called her into relationship with Him, and she gave Him her heart. She's always been His, and He alone has the right to determine her path and purpose. I was part of that path and purpose here on earth, but that part of her life is over and I must let go of it. I must "forgive" God, acknowledging that I don't have any real say in His plan for her. He didn't have to ask my permission. She is <u>His</u>.

That was my treasure to surrender—living in my past with Lauren, holding onto my plans for her—so that I could move forward in life and embrace *God's* plans for her. I wrote:

> *Lord, I don't know if I can let her go like this, even though she's been taken from me. I can't understand this life without her in it, so I'm having a lot of trouble accepting it. I don't know if I can do the rest of life here like this. Honestly, I don't want to. I don't want to accept or live with this loss. Help me to be able to give her up and acknowledge that she's always been Yours. Help me to accept Your right to determine her path and mine, without my permission. I'm holding out my fisted hand to You. Make me able to open it and release her to You.*

I tried to give God my plastic pink pearls: my past with Lauren, and the future I wanted with her. But I was having a hard time letting go. It felt like leaving Lauren behind, moving farther and farther away from her. I needed a glimpse of the real pink pearls God had in store for me.

7/18/2008, PM

> *These plastic pearls are no longer mine. But I'm still trying to hang on to them. What does God have for me in their place? What are His real pearls? Show me, Lord.*

By this time, we had come home from camp and left again the same day for a family reunion. We met my parents, my brother and sister, and their families that night at a hotel. A get-together with my mom's extended family was planned for the next day. At dinner that night, the adults sat at a big round table, the kids at a table next to us. While we were eating, I noticed across the table that my sister, Vicki, was wearing a very pretty beaded necklace. I asked her about it, and she said it was a gift she just got from a friend who bought it on an overseas trip. It was the first time Vicki had worn it. When I asked her what kind of beads they were, she answered, "These are freshwater pearls." My heart nearly stopped—they were pink.

The next day, we met for lunch with all the cousins, aunts and uncles. As we sat around in groups talking, I overheard my cousin Krista say that her husband liked to give her pearls. She had strands of pearls in several different colors. I looked over at her and noticed that she was wearing a beautiful *pink* pearl necklace. "Are those real pearls?" I asked her. She smiled and told me yes, they were real.

Funny thing was, when I greeted her earlier that day, I didn't notice her pink pearls. She had cried and hugged my neck, because we hadn't seen each other since the accident— she lives in Alaska and couldn't be at Lauren's memorial service. In fact, I rarely see her at all. But here, God had arranged for me to see pink pearls He brought all the way from Alaska, and I had missed them! So He made sure to call my attention to them. How like Him.

The world and everything in it truly does belong to our God. And He still moves heaven and earth to lavish His love on His children.

I was so stunned by the nature of this unlikely and visible message from God that I couldn't yet express it to anyone.[14] I had to talk with God about it first, to process it all. So, that evening as we drove home, I wrote:

7/19/2008

Two real pink pearl necklaces in two days, immediately following Zane's story and challenge.

Tonight, I remembered a desperate prayer I voiced through my tears Thursday night among the trees outside the tabernacle. "Lord, I need You. I need to feel You holding me, physically, tangibly. You alone." I wanted an unmistakable touch from Jesus. I watched the sky, hoping He might give me a visible sign of His presence. Then, the thought left my mind. Until today, after seeing the only two real pink pearl necklaces I've ever seen in my life...That is the most visible and tangible touch from my Savior I can imagine outside of physically being in His arms someday. And it's the promise of the real pink pearls He has for me when I give Him my plastic ones.

My real pink pearls? The <u>peace</u> of knowing I can give Lauren fully to Jesus without being afraid of losing her. The <u>healing</u> that will come as I rest

---

[14]   Though I mentioned the possible significance of my sister's pink pearls to her when I first saw them, it was only later that I shared the full story with her. I sent a written copy to my cousin and have shared it with those closest to Lauren as well, so that they could have the promise of the pink pearls: they too are moving closer to Lauren each day. Every time I share the story and people respond with awe, I'm reminded what a striking sign from God it was.

*in His promise of our future perfect relationship.
The <u>courage</u> to live the rest of my days here with
joy and anticipation. The <u>assurance</u> that **I won't
be leaving her behind, but will be moving
closer to her every day that I serve the Lord
with gladness.***

To make sure I wouldn't forget His promise in the pink
pearls, God gave me two confirmations. The first came
during an appointment with my chiropractor one week later.
It had been almost ten months since the last time I went, but
I could no longer ignore my worsening back pain.

Walking into the office the day of my appointment, I
decided not to talk about Lauren. It tended to ruin people's
day, and I hadn't yet learned to use it as a testimony to God's
faithfulness. So I didn't often bring it up with people who
didn't know.

The problem was, because I hadn't been to see him in
ten months, the doctor asked me about changes, stress, or
injuries I might have had since I saw him last. I could have
skirted around that question, but then he asked if there had
been any deaths in our family. I told him about Lauren.

After telling me how sorry he was, he asked me one
more question. "Did she know the Lord?" He is a strong
follower of Christ, so I knew what he was asking. I said yes,
absolutely. And this is what he said:

> "I have two words for you. First, she's not lost,
> because we know where she is. Second, don't be
> afraid to move forward. She's not in your past,
> but in your future, and every step you take will
> be toward her and not away from her."

I could hardly believe what he was saying! The very thing God told me with pink pearls. No one in the past five months of grieving had said anything remotely like this to me. Yet here was this doctor who just found out about Lauren, and those were the words God gave him to tell me.

The second confirmation came straight from Scripture:

> *"All honor to the God and Father of our Lord Jesus Christ, for it is by his boundless mercy that God has given us the privilege of being born again. Now we live with a **wonderful expectation** because Jesus Christ rose again from the dead. **For God has reserved a priceless inheritance for his children. It is kept in heaven for you, pure and undefiled, beyond the reach of change and decay.** And God, in his mighty power, will protect you until you receive this salvation, because you are trusting him. It will be revealed on the last day for all to see."*

1 Peter 1:3-5

I've written beside this passage the words "real pink pearls," because these verses are the very promise God gave me through them. All who know Christ have an untouchable inheritance kept for them—eternal life in His presence and the restoration of all things. My future relationship with Lauren is secure—as secure as each of us is in the love of our Savior.

The promise in the real pink pearls was exactly what I needed to be able to open my fist and give my plastic ones to God. The only way I could move forward in life here was to see that I'm moving closer to Lauren. She's in my future, so I'm not moving away from her in the past. Reading over my journal to prepare for writing this section, I could see that now, almost three years later, I have received the peace, healing, courage, and assurance to live with joy and anticipation. I'm getting closer and closer to my real pink pearls—eternal life and reunion with Lauren in the presence of Jesus—that God is keeping in heaven for me.

At the time, however, this was only my first step in moving toward the future. The grief was still too fresh, the pain too raw, and Satan's lies too persistent. There was still a battle ahead.

The Land of Promises

The Holy Spirit was teaching me much about the promises of heaven and Christ's return to restore all things. He had given me a sign of real pink pearls to let me know Lauren is in my future. I wanted so badly to silence the questions and fear that made me reluctant to fully embrace His promises. So God took me to the story of the Israelites in the book of Deuteronomy.

If you've ever read Deuteronomy, you may have realized that it often gets a bad rap. Maybe because of its name, or maybe because it comes right after Leviticus and Numbers, many people think it's a dry and boring book of rules. But it's really a call from God to His people to choose life instead of death. And the life He describes for them is abundant and beautiful. In fact, it's a physical analogy of the spiritual abundance and beauty of life in Jesus Christ that we can have today. It also foreshadows the eternal abundance and beauty of the true promised land—the new heavens and new earth.

So there I was, reading through Deuteronomy, still trying not to drown in the apathy caused by my grief. Chapter one begins as the Israelites are once again standing at the border of the promised land. They'd wandered in the desert for 40 years because they were afraid to go in when God commanded the first time. Moses had tried to encourage them the first time, saying, *"Don't be afraid! The Lord your God is going before you. He will fight for you just as you saw Him do in Egypt. And you saw how the Lord your God cared for you again and again here in the wilderness, just as a father cares for his child. Now He has brought you to this place"* (1:29-31). But they were too afraid and refused to go in. And suddenly I saw myself.

7/22/2008

I've been in the wilderness, under the care of my loving Father. Over and over, He provided for me, protected me, and fought for me. He has taken me to the mountain, revealing His awesome, unmistakable presence to me. Now He's calling me forward, and He promises to go before me and fight for me. He told me not to fear that I will leave Lauren behind, because she's not in the past. She's in the future, in the Promised Land that the Lord is calling me to. Will I follow Him in love, trust, and obedience? Or will I disobey, letting fear keep me from following Him?

Lord, You told me I have nothing to fear. Fear is not from You, but from Satan. Bind him and cast him out. And fill me with the truth of Your promises. "For God has not given us a spirit of fear and timidity, but of power, love and self-discipline" (2 Timothy 1:7).

The promised land for New Testament believers is salvation in Jesus Christ and eternal life with Him in His Kingdom. We enter His eternal Kingdom the moment we give our lives to Him. And we anticipate its full coming at Christ's return. He will renew all creation, establishing His Kingdom in the new heavens and new earth, our promised land. For now, we must live in the Land of His Promises:

"Since you have been raised to new life with Christ, set your sights on the realities of heaven, where Christ sits at God's right hand in the place of honor and power. Let heaven fill your thoughts. Do not think only about things down here on earth. For you died when Christ died, and your real life is hidden with Christ in God."

Colossians 3:1-3

We may live here on earth right now, but we're already citizens of heaven, and we need to live like it. That doesn't mean to have our heads in the clouds, just biding our time until we get to heaven. It means letting our citizenship in heaven affect the way we live right now, as ambassadors of the Kingdom. This keeps us from investing in the worthless treasures of here and now, motivating us instead to invest in the treasures of heaven—God and His people.

Because I wasn't living securely in God's promises, I was continually fighting fear, doubt, and apathy. I had no desire to be here on earth or to invest here. I just wanted my faith to be made sight, jumping right over all the pain I was sure I would face every day of my life. But I kept waking up here.

It finally dawned on me that if God still had me here, there was a reason. There must still be something He wanted me to do for His Kingdom. And if that was so, I couldn't remain on the border, refusing to enter the Land of His Promises.

Then I read Deuteronomy 9 and realized that God's call to enter His promises was for more than my own healing. In this chapter, Moses was reminding the people of the time he came down the mountain with the Ten Commandments and found them worshipping a golden calf. God had been so angry that He told Moses He would destroy them and make a new nation from Moses' descendants. This was Moses' reply:

> *"If you destroy these people, the Egyptians will say, 'The Lord destroyed them because He wasn't able to bring them into the land He had sworn to give them.'"*

v. 28a

8/13/2008

Wow. This convicts me. If I refuse to enter the Land of Promises that God has given me, I could hurt His reputation among unbelievers. Instead of being a powerful witness to God's faithfulness, I could make some who are watching think that God isn't real or isn't able to do what He promises.

The last thing I wanted to do was dishonor God by refusing to believe His promises. People were watching. And God was showing up. How could I ever live as though He wasn't? I determined then and there that no matter how fierce the battle, I would defeat my giants and enter the land God was giving me.

> *God freed me from slavery in "Egypt" when He saved me from sin and death. I was learning to live in freedom in so many areas of my life. But then I was plunged into the wilderness of terrible testing. From here, it's a daily fight for survival. Yet God faithfully cares for me one day at a time. That's not where the story should end, though. It's not complete until I enter the Land of His Promises. I can get there, to an extent in this life, by faith. I can live in Christ's promises by believing them and receiving the peace they offer. But only at death or His returning will I enter by sight. Until then, I must fight the giants that try to keep me out of His Land of Promises.*

> *"Hear O Israel! Today you are about to cross the Jordan River to occupy the land belonging to nations much greater and more powerful than you...But the Lord your God will cross over ahead of you like a devouring fire to destroy them. He will subdue them so that you will quickly conquer them and drive them out, just as the Lord has promised."*

> *Deuteronomy 9:1, 3*

> *Lord Jesus, go before me and destroy the giants that keep me from occupying Your Land of Promises.*

And He did go before me, straight into a battle with the fiercest of enemies.

Chapter 6—The Battle: Fear and Doubt

"I prayed to the Lord, and he answered me,
freeing me from all my fears.
Those who look to him for help will be radiant with joy;
no shadow of shame will darken their faces."
Psalm 34:4-5

My battle with fear and doubt began on February 11, 2008. From the first day of grief, fear was my constant companion. At first, I couldn't figure out what I was afraid of. But gradually, as my jumbled thoughts took on a little bit of order, I saw it was doubt that made me afraid. Questions bombarded me.

> *What if God's not really there? And if He's not,*
> *then Lauren hasn't gone to be with Him. She's*
> *just gone. How can she be gone? Will I ever see*
> *my little girl again? If I won't, I can't survive this.*
> *What if the Bible isn't really true? Can I believe*

> *any of God's promises? Am I alone? How will I*
> *ever make it through one more day without my*
> *daughter? What if I have to live here 50 more*
> *years separated from her?*

Be Still

So many questions clambered in my head, demanding my attention, that I couldn't shove them far enough away. They haunted me day and night. I had to get answers or I'd go crazy. Literally.

2/25/2008

> *"Then Job replied to the Lord, 'I am nothing—*
> *how could I ever find the answers? I will put my*
> *hand over my mouth in silence. I have said too*
> *much already. I have nothing more to say.'"*

Job 40:3-5

> *I've been talking to myself out of my pain so much*
> *that I haven't taken time to still my mind and*
> *listen to You. Please forgive me Lord, and still my*
> *mind. You "work for those who wait for You."*

"Be still and know that I am God!" Psalm 46:10

"Be still and know that I am God" –Lauren's favorite scripture. How many times before had the Holy Spirit used her life, words, and faith to speak to me? I needed to start listening. To do that I had to be still.

From the beginning, I knew Satan was at the root of all my doubts. He shoved lie after lie in front of me, hoping I would take hold of them and separate myself from the truth.

But God told me in no uncertain terms that He was fighting the enemy for me:

> *"The eternal God is your refuge, and His everlasting arms are under you. He thrusts out the enemy before you; it is He who cries, 'Destroy them!'"*
>
> Deuteronomy 33:27

> *"Cast your burden upon the Lord, and He will sustain you; He will never allow the righteous to be shaken."*
>
> Psalm 55:22

> *"The Lord will fight for you; you need only to be still."*
>
> Exodus 14:14, NIV

Be still. Lord Jesus, You keep telling me this. Thank You! My questions and pain get so loud at times that I know I'm not being still or trusting You. When I'm not, I try to fight this battle on my own. Help me to worship You today, filling this house and my heart with praise to You. For You have said, "Only in returning to Me and waiting for Me will you be saved. In quietness and confidence is your strength" (Isaiah 30:15a). Help me not to be like the Israelites who "would have none of it" (v.15b). Quiet my heart with confidence in You to fight this battle for me. I place my trust in You today. I surrender everything to You—my pain and sorrow, my grief, my questions and whys, any lies of Satan that are still stuck in my mind, my thoughts, my feelings, any anger, my words, everything Lord. Take over, cleanse, heal. Fill me, fight for me. I need You.

Believe

Although it was going to be a long battle, God promised He would go before me. He would defeat the enemy, and make sure I wasn't destroyed, even though my faith was being violently shaken. Then He reminded me of what I could believe. He showed me scripture after scripture that promised I would see my daughter again. I shared what I learned in depth in an earlier chapter, but here are some of the first precious promises the Holy Spirit gave me:

"But as for me, I know that my Redeemer lives, and that he will stand upon the earth at last. And after my body has decayed, yet in my body I will see God! I will see him for myself. Yes, I will see him with my own eyes. I am overwhelmed at the thought!"

Job 19:25-27

"For you will not leave my soul among the dead or allow your godly one to rot in the grave. You will show me the way of life, granting me the joy of your presence and the pleasures of living with you forever."
Psalm 16:10-11

"Yet we have this assurance; Those who belong to God will live; Their bodies will rise again!

Those who sleep in the earth
Will rise up and sing for joy!
For God's light of life will fall like dew
On his people in the place of the dead!"

Isaiah 26:19

"As for you, go your way until the end. You will
rest, and then at the end of days, you will rise
again to receive the inheritance set aside for you."

Daniel 12:13

And these are just the Old Testament passages that speak of the resurrection of the body. It's a far less developed truth in the Old Testament, but it *is* there, presented so concretely. God showed me what He needed me to focus on—His promises of life—in the face of death. He opened my eyes to things greater than what I could physically see. This wasn't denial of reality, it was seeing *true* reality.

The Holy Spirit also showed me the teachings of Jesus concerning those who have died:

"But now, as to whether the dead will be raised—
even Moses proved this when he wrote about the
burning bush. Long after Abraham, Isaac, and
Jacob had died, he referred to the Lord as 'the
God of Abraham, the God of Isaac, and the God
of Jacob.' So he is the God of the living, not the
dead. They are all alive to him."

Luke 20:37-38

Matthew records God's words at the burning bush more like Moses did in Exodus 3: *"I* am (present tense) *the God of*

Abraham, Isaac, and Jacob" (see Matthew 22:32 and Exodus 3:6). Jesus, as God, knew what had been communicated to Moses that day. Those who belong to God are eternally alive.

As I write this, I've just received word that my close friend Rebecca has lung cancer, and it's in her lymph nodes. She's a beloved child of God, and I know He will heal her. Whether it's on this side of heaven or the other, she's eternally alive. There's no death sentence for those who know Christ. What hope, to be able to look death in the face and see only life! It's as Jesus said in John 5:24: *"I assure you, those who listen to my message and believe in God who sent me have eternal life. They will never be condemned for their sins, but they have **already** passed from death into life."*

This was the verse my sister gave me the first week after Lauren went to heaven. She wrote it out for me and said, "Lauren never experienced death. She went straight from life here to life in heaven with Jesus." How right she is! Though Lauren's body died, her unique self—her soul—never did. Jesus said this very thing Himself:

> *"I am the resurrection and the life. Anyone who believes in me will live, even after dying. Everyone who lives in me and believes in me will **never ever** die."*

> John 11:25-26

And, Jesus conquered even the death of our bodies when He rose from the dead.

As I read Jesus' words of resurrection hope and life to Martha in John 11, I also heard His question to her, *"Do you believe this, Martha?"* (v. 26b) He was asking me too. *Do you believe this, Alicia?*

Jesus asked Martha this question four days after her brother Lazarus died. He was asking her to see life in the face of death—the life only He could give. He was asking me too, as I faced incomprehensible loss in my daughter's death, to see life instead.

3/3/2008

Do I believe this? Is Jesus the resurrection and the life? Will those who believe in Him live, even though they die? For the first time in seven years, I've asked these questions deep inside. I confess that Lauren's sudden departure from this world, her physical death, has shaken me to the core. I've questioned everything I believe. It's weird though, because I've also lived my faith more boldly than ever before. I have no fear of sharing the Gospel or living to please God rather than men. It's only these little barbed thoughts and fleeting fears that shoot through my mind and cause me to doubt. In every other way, my faith is real and God's strength is working in my weakness to bring glory to Himself. Those barbs and fears are nothing but insidious lies of the enemy. I must daily surrender myself—all my pain and brokenness—to God. I must allow Him to be my fortress and refuge, to repair the walls of my life, so that my enemy can't get a foothold in me.

So to answer Jesus' question: "Do you believe this?"—that He is the resurrection and the life, that all who believe in Him will never die—I

> *can say with growing confidence, "YES!" I believe*
> *Jesus, I believe <u>in</u> Him. I'll live every moment He*
> *chooses to give me here on earth for Him. I'll also*
> *live with Him forever, in the company of Lauren*
> *and all who love Him.*

Even this early in my grief, I see evidence in my journals of the great battle I had with Satan's lies, a battle that would come to a head almost a year and a half later. So while I could say, and mean, that I believed Jesus, the struggle for my faith was far from over. For now, I held on to every promise in God's Word.

The Joy to Come

Jesus made it very clear in John 6 why He had come. *"Spend your energy seeking the eternal life that I, the Son of Man, can give you. For God the Father has sent me **for that very purpose**"* (v. 27). He came to do the Father's work: *"For it is my Father's will that all who see his Son and believe in him should have eternal life—that I should raise them at the last day"* (v.40). This work was the salvation of the believer's soul, and the resurrection of the believer's body.

God's words through Paul and Peter give more detail to the promise of eternal life for believers:

> *"And now, brothers and sisters, I want you to know*
> *what will happen to the Christians who have died*
> *so you will not be full of sorrow like people who*
> *have no hope. For since we believe that Jesus died*
> *and was raised to life again, we also believe that*
> *when Jesus comes, God will bring back with Jesus all*
> *the Christians who have died…Then, together with*
> *them, we who are still alive and remain on the earth*

will be caught up in the clouds to meet the Lord in the air and remain with him forever. So comfort and encourage each other with these words."

1 Thessalonians 4:13-14, 17-18

"Now we live with a wonderful expectation because Jesus Christ rose again from the dead. For God has reserved a priceless inheritance for his children. It is kept in heaven for you, pure and undefiled, beyond the reach of change and decay. And God, in his mighty power, will protect you until you receive this salvation, because you are trusting him. It will be revealed on the last day for all to see. So be truly glad! There is wonderful joy ahead, even though it is necessary for you to endure many trials for a while."

1 Peter 1:3-6

It was here in Peter's words that I first began to see a light at the end of the tunnel of grief, "wonderful joy ahead." It was a long way off, seemingly unattainable at the time. But Paul spoke of joy ahead also, and I clung to those words of hope with everything in me.

"For our present troubles are quite small and won't last very long. Yet they produce for us an immeasurably great glory that will last forever! So we don't look at the troubles we can see right now; rather, we look forward to what we have not yet seen. For the troubles we see will soon be over, but the joys to come will last forever."

2 Corinthians 4:17-18

No matter what trouble came into my life, I had to hold onto the promise that in light of eternity it would soon be over, too small even to compare with the joy to come.

But these passages also began to raise questions. Why are trials necessary, as Peter says? How do they produce for us the immeasurably great glory that Paul talks about? Over the next two and a half years, God would teach me much in answer to these questions, and I will share it in a later chapter. From the beginning, though, I knew this: *"These trials are only to test your faith, to show that it is strong and pure. It is being tested as fire tests and purifies gold—and your faith is far more precious to God than mere gold"* (*1 Peter 1:7a*). Oh, how I wanted my faith to come through this trial, strong and pure.

Battle Assignments

The battle raged on, the fires of grief testing my faith more than I could have ever imagined. Along the way, God did as He promised: He fought for me, abundantly pouring out His words of promise like I shared above. But every now and then, He gave me a battle assignment of my own.

Less than a month after Lauren went to heaven, a man Scott worked with sat in Scott's office and shared this with him:

> "Lauren was prepared, so when Satan saw an opportunity to destroy your family, God allowed him to take it. But instead of destroying you, he unwittingly and unwillingly brought great victory to the Kingdom of God. He is greatly regretting the day he messed with your family and your God."

We know that God is completely in control of all things, so Satan didn't do something on February 11th that surprised God. God didn't then have to "fix" or rearrange His plan. Satan doesn't have that kind of control; ultimately God allowed Lauren to come home that day because it was the best possible plan, not plan B. But Satan is still the enemy who tries to destroy us. And God called us that day to live the rest of our lives bringing victory for His Kingdom out of the very thing Satan used to try to defeat us.

3/4/2008

I want to live the rest of my days here on earth making Satan rue the day he ever messed with God's children. I want him to know every day that what he meant for harm, God is using for incredible good. He tried to destroy us and our witness. But what he did instead was bring great glory to our God and draw many to Him.

Jesus, I pray that You will continue the massive ripple effect started by Lauren's life and death on this earth, just like You've done with many other untimely deaths. I pray that any time Satan tries this again, You will continue to use him to destroy himself. Put a fire in my heart, today and every day, to bring great victory for Your Kingdom out of this terrible tragedy.

"To all who mourn in Israel, He will give beauty for ashes, joy instead of mourning, praise instead of despair. For the Lord has planted them like strong and graceful oaks for His own glory."

Isaiah 61:3

"Precious (important and no light matter) in the sight of the Lord is the death of His saints (His loving ones)."

Psalm 116:15 (AMP)

Thank You, Lord that You don't take Lauren's death lightly, and that You will avenge her and all Your saints. You take it very personally when Satan attacks those You love. I know You will cast Satan into eternal punishment on the last day, but You've revealed to me how You punish him every day right now by turning his attacks back on him. You will destroy his kingdom here on earth little by little as You bring many victories for Your Kingdom out of such tragedy.

Another assignment God gave me concerned my focus. What I chose to dwell on would make a huge difference in the battle for my faith.

2/26/2008

"Just thinking about my troubles and my lonely wandering makes me miserable. That's all I ever think about, and I am depressed. Then I remember something that fills me with hope. The Lord's kindness never fails! If He had not been merciful, we would have been destroyed. The Lord can always be trusted to show mercy each morning. Deep in my heart I say, 'The Lord is all I need; I can depend on Him!'"

Lamentations 3:19-24(CEV)

God is showing me that I've been dwelling on the accident, the "if onlys," the irreversibility of our loss, and the ache of missing her. Just thinking about these things "makes me miserable." When "that's all I ever think about," "I am depressed." And I quench the Holy Spirit in me. I've stopped the flow of His character and power in me. Somehow, I have to start dwelling on the truth of who God is and of His promises to us. I have to begin to focus on the promises that He has fulfilled for Lauren. "And he himself has promised us this: eternal life" (1 John 2:25). I want to remember and dwell on this promise and many others, letting God restore my hope and give me peace.

Lord, fill me with Your Holy Spirit today. There's a huge hole in my heart that I need You to pour Yourself into continually. Help me Lord, to dwell on Your tender mercies and Your promises of victory over death. Keep me from thinking— dwelling—on what I lost. Instead fill me with assurance of <u>what Lauren has gained</u>.

Fear for Lauren

Part of my battle with fear concerned what happened to Lauren in the accident. Because of it, I couldn't focus on what she gained that day. I had memories of the scene, and added to that were mental images I formed from the information we got from the police and medical examiner. Just imagining what Lauren might have gone through in her last moments here filled my "mother's heart" with horror.

3/5/2008

Lord, I need to give you my memories and images of the accident, the facts of what happened, the *fear I feel for my little girl. It makes my heart pound, my skin burn, and my stomach turn. I don't know how to deal with all my mind knows and remembers. I have no peace when I remember that day. Jesus, show me what <u>You</u> saw.*

"Don't be afraid of those who want to kill you. They can only kill your body; <u>they cannot touch your soul</u>. Fear only God, who can destroy both soul and body in hell. Not even a sparrow, worth only half a penny, can fall to the ground without your Father knowing it. And the very hairs of your head are all numbered. So don't be afraid; you are more valuable to him than a whole flock of sparrows."

Matthew 10:28-31

Lord Jesus, You were completely aware of what happened to Lauren. And You were there with her. Only her body was killed, her soul wasn't touched. Help me not to be afraid for her Lord. Please give me peace in knowing You were with her there and You still are. She loves You and belongs to You and now she's with You. "If anyone acknowledges me publicly here on earth, I will openly acknowledge that person before my Father in heaven" (Matthew 10:32). Lauren acknowledged You publicly in so many ways here on earth. Thank You for showing me that You acknowledged her before Your Father when she arrived in heaven that day. What a glorious day it must have been for her as she saw You face to face. I know she worshiped You, and then was received by Your Father.

Jesus, I pray that You will help me add the things You saw and did that day to my memories. Expand what I know to include what You know. Remove the turmoil of my own memories and knowledge, replacing it with the peace of knowing what You know.

Within three days, the Holy Spirit answered this prayer. He began in Psalm 91:

> "*'Because he loves me,' says the Lord, 'I will rescue him; I will protect him, for he acknowledges my name. He will call upon me, and I will answer him; I will be with him in trouble, I will deliver him and honor him. With long life will I satisfy him and show him my salvation.'*"

v.14-15 (NIV)

Verses like this bothered me greatly after the accident, because I struggled to accept that God didn't *physically* protect Lauren. I knew she was eternally safe and protected, but why didn't God honor her with long life here? She loved Him. She acknowledged His name. And beyond that, it hurt terribly to think of the physical trauma she endured that day.

In the accident, Lauren's car rolled four times, ejecting her through her window on the last roll. The car then rolled on top of her, compressing her chest so that she asphyxiated. It happened in minutes, but the thought of those last moments were more than I could bear. Why didn't God protect her? All He would've had to do was keep the car from rolling the last time. Or make sure she was thrown clear of where it would land. That's all it would have taken, because she didn't have a broken bone or even a scratch.

I'm giving these details so that God's answer to me in Psalm 91:14 will become obvious. I cried out to God to help me see what He saw that day, to understand how He protected her when He didn't do it physically. He led me to dig deeper into this verse in its original language. Here's what I found:

> Love—to be attached to, love, have pleasure in, delight in. Has the sense of joining together, adhering to, cleaving.
>
> Acknowledge—to perceive, understand, know, discern...The sense of "knowing" someone includes God, although God is too great to be fully understood.
>
> Call upon—to cry out, call, to name; essentially denotes the enunciation of a specific message which is usually addressed to a specific recipient and intended to elicit a specific response.
>
> Deliver—to draw off, draw out, extricate...take off; to rescue, be drawn out.
>
> Salvation (Ye suah)—help, deliverance, salvation, victory.[15]

3/9/2008

The picture I see from these definitions begins with Lauren's commitment to Jesus. Her journals are full of her love for Him and her desire to follow Him every day, to shine for Him in this dark world. In

---

[15]   Spiros Zodhiates, Th.D., et al., *Hebrew-Greek Key Word Study Bible, NIV* (Chattanooga, TN: AMG Publishers, 1996).

so many ways she acknowledged Him. Her trust was in Jesus to save her. She sought to know and understand God better each day. Lauren called out to Jesus that day because He was already her Savior. She called to Him to rescue her. He drew her out, extricated her from underneath that car and took her immediately to heaven. "Today you will be with me in Paradise." And so she is. God fulfilled His promise of salvation in her life. Ye suah, the Hebrew word for salvation, is the name Jesus in Greek. She received Jesus, her salvation, in full that day.

I wish I could adequately describe the joy that flooded my heart as I wrote this. I received such a vivid and specific answer to my request to see past what I knew of Lauren's experience that day. What a tender, loving God we have! He let me see that He was there with my baby when I couldn't be. He pulled her out from beneath that car. She didn't remain trapped there—what I feared most of her experience—but was pulled to safety and ushered home in the arms of her Savior.

My friend Andrea confirmed this very picture. She told me, not long after, that God had shown her He was with Lauren that day, as always. And in that field, He pulled her into His arms to take her home.

Months later, because my heart still needed reminding so often in those days, the Holy Spirit gave me another picture with a song:

When all of a sudden,
I am unaware of these afflictions eclipsed by glory,
And I realize just how beautiful You are,

135

And how great Your affections are for me...[16]
　　　　　—"How He Loves," John Mark McMillan

Listening to those lyrics, I heard them from Lauren's point of view on February 11th. That day, as the song later says, Heaven met earth in an unforeseen (at least to us) kiss, and the afflictions of the accident were eclipsed by the glory of Jesus Christ. Lauren saw His beauty and His affection as He called her to Him. In the moments the accident occurred, heaven met earth. That field became a door from this world into the next. Any regrets or fear she had were instantly gone as she turned to Him and went Home.

As late as the fall of 2010, the Holy Spirit continued to tell me what Lauren really experienced that day. Andrea (the friend who received the same vision about the accident that I did) brought me a book called *The Furious Longing of God* by Brennan Manning. She had marked a chapter for me to read. Near the end of it, Manning tells the story of visiting a home in Louisiana that cared for lepers. He was called to come pray with a woman who, as he described her, had been very beautiful before leprosy took her fingers and parts of her face. Yolanda was in the last stages of leprosy, and was dying alone. Her husband had left her, forbidding their children to have anything to do with her.

On the day Manning visited, he anointed Yolanda with oil and prayed for her. He turned away to put the lid back on the bottle of oil, and the room filled with radiant light. He thought it was a ray of sunshine coming into the room, but as he turned to Yolanda, he was stunned by the light on her face. It radiated through the whole room so brightly that he had to

---

[16]　John Mark McMillan, "How He Loves," (John Mark McMillan, 2005).

shield his face. He asked her why she was so happy, and she said that the Abba of Jesus had just told her He would take her Home that day. Through tears, Manning asked her what the Abba of Jesus said. She spoke these words:

"Come now, my love. My lovely one, come.

For you, the winter has passed,
the snows are over and gone,
the flowers appear in the land,
the season of joyful songs has come.

The cooing of the turtledove
is heard in our land.

Come now, my love. My Yolanda, come.

Let me see your face. And let me hear your voice,
For your voice is sweet
And your face is beautiful.

Come now, my love, my lovely one, come.

from Song of Solomon 2:10-14 (NJB)

Manning recognized this passage. French biblical scholar Pierre Benoit believed these were the words God the Father spoke to Jesus as He died. Benoit wrote that God revealed this to him after 35 years of praying and meditating on the death of Christ.

Six hours after Manning's visit, Yolanda went Home to be with the Lord. Later that day, he discovered that she'd been illiterate. She never read the Bible or any other book. And Manning didn't read the words from Song of Solomon to her on any visit.[17]

I wept as the words of Song of Solomon 2 washed over me like healing balm, knowing that truly "precious in His sight is the death of His saints," including my little girl's. Andrea and I both believe the Holy Spirit clearly showed us, then confirmed, what Lauren experienced that day when Jesus met her and called her Home to Him.

Lauren's Song

Other grief-initiated fears gripped me for a long time. One morning, I received reassurance for fear in general from a truly surprising place. While going through the many folders of pictures Lauren had put on our home computer, I discovered, tucked into one, a video she'd made. I'd never seen it before. She recorded it at the piano, playing and singing a song that I heard her practice many times. When I asked her once what song it was, she told me she and a friend at school wrote it. I always enjoyed hearing her play it because it sounded like something from the radio. But I never paid attention to the lyrics until I opened the video file that day, weeks after the accident. As I watched and listened to my daughter sing, the message went straight to my heart:

> Her world is crashing down
> She knows that He'll be there
> Everything's changing now
> Where does she go from here?

---

[17] Brennan Manning, *The Furious Longing of God* (Colorado Springs: David C. Cook, 2009), adapted from 51-56.

She feels that she's alone
There's nobody at home
Who understands her pain
Why can't things stay the same?
Why can't things stay the same?

Trust in Him, He'll always be.
Trust in Him is what you say to me.

(After a second verse and chorus):

Her world is crashing down
She knows that He'll be there
He'll always be around
There's nothing to fear.
　　　　　—Lauren Crawley and Amy Strom

I couldn't believe what I was hearing. My own daughter was describing my world and telling me there was nothing to fear. I could trust the Lord in my pain and in the rubble of my life. How had God arranged this gift for me, from my very own, wise-beyond-her-years daughter? What a gift of love!

Defeating the Enemy

It took a year and a half for the Holy Spirit to break the iron grip that fear and doubt had on me. Over time, I forgot it was Satan's voice telling me all the lies that God was not there. The lies wore me down until I was completely oppressed. The battle for my freedom finally came to a head in July 2009. And what a fight it was.

My human solution to the lies I now heard as my own thoughts was to talk myself out of them. I read everything

I could about the evidence for God, thinking I just needed to shore up my faith with all the proof I could. But as important as it is to know what our faith is based upon, this didn't address the real root of my problem. No matter what factual arguments I pursued or the proof of personal encounters with God I experienced, I couldn't drown out the voice in my head. At times, I even thought, *if this never goes away, I'm going to have to give up believing.* I knew it wasn't logical, but I couldn't find any other way out.

Finally, I took it to the Lord.

> *Lord God, I lay before You my greatest fear—that You're not really there. It's my point of greatest weakness, because my sanity depends on You and Your victory at the cross. Victory over grief only comes for me if You <u>are</u>. The rest of my life stands or falls on this, and this alone.*
>
> *What baffles me is that You speak, over and over, to me. I recognize and listen to Your voice. You continue to speak words of life to me abundantly, but my natural, sinful self won't fully accept it. <u>Everything</u> tells me You are there and You are the truth: reason, science, logic, discovery and above all, <u>YOUR WORD</u>.*

From that Word, the Holy Spirit finally broke through the deceptive oppression I was under. He showed me the true source of the thoughts I couldn't get rid of.

> *"There is no truth in him (Satan). When he lies, it is consistent with his character; for he is a liar and the father of lies."*

> John 8:44

From John 10:

"The thief's purpose is to steal, kill and destroy. My purpose is to give life in all its fullness."

v. 10

"I (Jesus) know my sheep, and they know me... they listen to my voice."

v. 14b, 16b

"They won't follow a stranger; they will run from him because they don't recognize his voice."

v. 5

It was the voice of the liar, the stranger, that kept saying, "He's not there. You're alone. You'll never see Lauren again." These thoughts didn't make sense, given everything I knew and was experiencing, and now I understood why. Because *they weren't my thoughts.* They were the voice of the stranger. I needed to run from him. And that's what I did, by running straight to Jesus.

7/11/2008

(exactly seventeen months after the accident)

I'm sick of the enemy's attacks! I am facing his lies once and for all. I hear them over and over. They won't go away. Lord, plaster Your Word all over my mind. Drive him away for good. I will <u>not</u> turn from You. Where else would I go? You alone

> *have the words of eternal life. And I believe them.*
> *Hide them in my heart. I am Yours.*

I stood in my bedroom that night and spoke aloud words of surrender to Christ. I rebuked Satan in the name of my Lord Jesus Christ, asking God to cast the enemy's voice out of my mind, my home and my life for good. I paced through the room, claiming Jesus as my Lord, and I took back the ground Satan was trying to take from me.

Immediately the lying words stopped. When I went to bed that night, I asked God to guard my mind with His words of truth.

The next morning, when we arrived at church, our friend Ray, affectionately known as "Papi," had on a shirt that said, *"No weapon formed against you shall prosper"* (Isaiah 54:17a, NKJV). I knew this was truth God provided for me to "plaster" all over my mind. I looked up the verse in my Bible and read it all:

> *"But in that coming day no weapon turned against you will succeed.* ***You will silence every voice raised up to accuse you.*** *These benefits are enjoyed by the servants of the Lord; their vindication will come from me. I, the Lord, have spoken!"*

> Isaiah 54:17

The gift of this verse that day still brings tears to my eyes. I knew it was God's promise that He had silenced the voice of the liar in my mind for good. But there was more.

The same morning, Scott showed me a verse he wanted to use in a ministry God was leading us to start. He read it from Romans 1: *"From the time the world was created, people have seen the earth and sky and all that God made.*

They can clearly see His invisible qualities—His eternal power and divine nature. So they have no excuse whatsoever for not knowing God" (v. 20).

More truth to guard my mind with. Because I'm a thinker (often an over-thinker), I've always felt threatened by the "enlightened" and "educated elite" in our culture who promote the attitude that anyone who believes in God is ignorant or deluded. This was the twist Satan often put on his lies to me: "You're viewed as stupid or crazy if you believe in God and eternal life." But God clearly states that the wisdom of this world is foolishness to Him, and that He will hide the truth from those who think they're wise, revealing it to the simple instead.

7/12/2009

Thank You Lord, for these passages to plaster my mind with. Just what I asked You for. You're so faithful! I didn't go looking for them—You put them before me. Words I wouldn't have searched for, but that You knew I would need. I don't deserve it, but will You please keep fighting for me?

I soon found out He did just that.

Two weeks after I asked God to keep fighting for me, Monty, a good friend of our family, approached me at church. He told me, very emotionally, that he had been heavily burdened for me for the last couple of weeks. He prayed for me every night, too burdened to sleep. This is how he described that time to me in an email:

"The first couple of nights I wondered if it were just me making something up in my head. While I knew it certainly would not hurt to be praying for you, was it merely my emotions that were keeping me awake and worked up? By the third night, as the urgency and desperateness of my pleas escalated, I sensed I was truly in full armor fighting a battle I did not understand... by the third and fourth night I could not even lie down. I paced back and forth from my bed to my bathroom and back, praying and quoting scripture. Occasionally, in my tiredness, I would think to myself, "I have prayed for hours, surely that is enough; I need to get some rest for tomorrow." I would lie down in bed and within seconds would literally get the "heebie-jeebies," my body had to move, it was like I was in a wrestling match and I would immediately get back up and start pacing again. A couple of times, I even had the image of me throwing full punches, as if I was warding off something in front of me. Is that weird, or what?

Desperate definitely describes my composure those nights. I have never felt so scared that if I messed up or eased up or stopped that I would let someone down in an eternal way. It literally felt that if I lost, your faith and very soul would be lost to us. That sounds extreme but I am trying to convey how surreally desperate this felt."

Of course, to me, it didn't sound extreme at all, because I was at the place where I knew if I couldn't silence the voice of doubt in my mind, I would just have to walk away from faith in God. I know I'm a child of God who will never be lost to Him, but that's only because *He* preserved my faith. And He used Monty to do it.

Two days after Monty told me his story, the Holy Spirit let me know my battle with doubt was over.

7/29/2009

When I sat down this morning to read, my Bible fell open to Revelation 12. I don't put much stock in where my Bible falls open as an indicator of what God wants to say to me. But this morning I felt very prompted to read the passage:

Revelation 12

"And the dragon lost the battle…Then I heard a loud voice shouting across the heavens, 'It has happened at last—the salvation and power and kingdom of our God, and the authority of His Christ! For the Accuser has been thrown down to earth—the one who accused our brothers and sisters before our God day and night. And they have defeated him because of the blood of the Lamb and because of their testimony. And they were not afraid to die."

v. 8, 10-11

The words rang in my mind: "The dragon lost the battle"—The Accuser is a defeated foe! Praise You, Lord!

Jesus accomplished this victory at the cross—"the blood of the Lamb." And now Satan was defeated in the battle for my faith. That was my testimony.

> *"Simon, Simon, Satan has asked to sift each of you like wheat. But I have pleaded in prayer for you, Simon, that your faith should not fail. So when you have repented and turned to me again, strengthen your brothers."*

Luke 22:31-32

Satan sifted me and tried to destroy my faith. But God sifted out my unbelief and the fear it caused instead. Now, as I repented and turned fully back to Him, He called me to strengthen others, to defeat Satan with my testimony of God's faithfulness. I can't wait to tell you how God continues to use the testimony of our lives to defeat Satan. He'll do the same for all who trust Him, in every circumstance, to fight for them and win the battle.

One last part of the story confirms the reality of the victory that God won for me over doubt and fear. Though it actually happened a week before that night I paced my bedroom, I didn't recognize it for what it was until after God set me free.

Jonathan and I went to my parents' house in Texas for the Fourth of July, because Scott and Jordan were out of town. As I drove, I heard a line in a song: "God is jealous for His own." I hadn't really been listening, but that line cut through my mental wanderings. I instantly got a vivid picture of myself, broken and crumpled on the ground, covered by the hands of God and surrounded by angels. *I fight for you,* rang through my heart and mind.

At the time, I saw this as a picture of what God had already done for me since the accident. And it was. Though Satan attacked me time after time, the Lord and His angels fought for me, protecting me when I lay broken and helpless on the ground. The Holy Spirit even gave me this verse later the same day: *"They will fight you, but they will fail. For I am with you, and I will take care of you. I, the Lord, have spoken!"* (Jeremiah 1:19)

But after I faced down the lies of Satan and learned of Monty's battle in prayer for me, I realized God had told me with that vision what He was *about* to do. So I shared it with Monty in an email. And he replied:

> "Wow! This was exactly what I pictured as I prayed for you incessantly on those nights...[It] is exactly the image I had and the reason I felt I was involved."

The Holy Spirit gave both of us the same picture of the battle He was about to wage. And then He faithfully delivered both of us through it. What a mighty warrior God we have! I'm so thankful He fought for me that July. It was the turning point of my faith through grief. He delivered me from the bondage of fear caused by Satan's oppressive lies, and I remain free from that fear to this day.

Fearless Faith

Only one fear remained: the fear of my earthly future. I knew my eternal future, and that of all my loved ones, was secure. But I wanted to be able to trust God fully again with the rest of my life here on earth.

The logic behind my fear went like this: I drew close to the Lord, pursuing Him with abandon, and I was blindsided by tragedy. Therefore, I wanted to be ready for it, should it come again. My way to be ready for it was to worry constantly about my loved ones. Somehow, fear and worry felt like being vigilant. If I thought and worried about everything bad that could happen, maybe it wouldn't happen, or at least I wouldn't be caught off guard again.

That was how I dealt with fear of the future for almost two and a half years. And it came to a head when Jonathan got his driving learner's permit. I knew the day was coming, and my plan for surviving it—watching him become independent and one day drive off without me—was just to "white-knuckle" my way through it. I resigned myself to living through it in fear.

But God called me to something greater one morning while I read the account of the disciples in a life-threatening storm on the Sea of Galilee. Matthew 8 tells how Jesus slept in the boat as the fierce storm struck. Waves were breaking over the boat, and Jesus slept on.

> *"The disciples went and woke him up, shouting, 'Lord, save us! We're going to drown!' Jesus responded, 'Why are you afraid? You have so little faith!'"*

> v. 25-26a

What I saw in this verse was that the disciples had faith to go to Jesus in their need, but not enough faith to keep them from being afraid. Jesus called them to greater faith—fearless faith. And I heard the Holy Spirit calling me to the same.

God didn't want me to fearfully get through the future. He wanted me to trust Him fear*less*ly. Days later, He called me to this again, with a verse from Proverbs 31:

> *"She is clothed with strength and dignity, and she laughs with no fear of the future."*

> v. 25

10/29/2010

The Lord keeps calling me to fearless faith, and I've resisted. I think I've just been hoping to "white-knuckle" my way through my greatest fear: letting Jonathan learn to drive and get his license. I'll do what I have to, to let him go, but only with great fear. But the Holy Spirit is calling me to a higher faith—real, fearless faith. "Trust in the Lord <u>with all your heart</u>." Can I honestly say I do that? I don't think so. And I'm not sure I want to, because if I do, it feels like completely letting go of control—as if fear and worry give me any control.

I mulled over this call to fearless faith for several weeks, wondering how to truly have it. Was I supposed to trust God not to let anything bad ever happen to my loved ones again? No, for He doesn't promise that. So what could I trust Him for? What would give me fearless faith as I faced my earthly future?

The Holy Spirit gave me the answer in 2 Corinthians 4. In this chapter, Paul talks about how others benefit when God's people suffer: they see the all-surpassing glory and power of Christ when He carries us through the difficult circumstances we face in this life.

11/18/2010

He is the answer—the only answer—to every need in every circumstance. If He shows Himself faithful—redeeming and restoring us through the worst life can bring—then others will be able to trust Him to get them through whatever they face.

People told us this very thing as they watched our family travel the dark road of grief. God assured them that if He could carry us through such pain and loss, He could carry them through what they were enduring. Then, as I reread my journal entry the next day, I finally saw it:

11/19/2010

> *The same is true for me. If He can get me through the worst thing in life—the loss of my daughter's presence here on earth—then He can get me through anything. And not only get me through it, but make me a conqueror over it. He can heal me, redeem the loss, and restore my hope, joy, and peace.*
>
> *My fearless faith, then, is in my all-powerful God. He alone keeps me secure and sane **through** all the trouble of this life.*

Joni Eareckson Tada (a quadriplegic for 40 years) says it this way:

> "The truth is, in this world it's a 100 percent guarantee that we *will* suffer. But at the same time, Jesus Christ is 100 percent certain to meet us, encourage us, comfort us, grace us with strength and perseverance, and yes, even restore joy in our lives. Your Savior is 100 percent certain to be with you through every challenge."[18]

I committed that day to walk in fearless faith one day at a time. Not faith that God would keep all suffering from my life, for He doesn't promise that. Instead, He promised that

---

[18]   Joni Eareckson Tada, *A Place of Healing* (Colorado Springs: David C. Cook, 2010), 144.

He would walk me through every bit of it, all the way to my eternal home. And there, suffering will finally be no more.

> *"Even when I walk*
> *through the dark valley of death,*
> *I will not be afraid,*
> *for you are close beside me.*
> *Your rod and your staff*
> *protect and comfort me."*
> Psalm 23:4

> *"He will wipe every tear from their eyes, and there will be no more death or sorrow or crying or pain. All these things are gone forever. And the one sitting on the throne said, 'Look, I am making everything new!'"*
>
> Revelation 21:4-5a

Chapter 7—Betrayal: Reconciling Love and Sovereignty

I grew up in an American middle-class home which provided all of my needs and many of my wants. We didn't have to do without. I felt safe, and I saw most everything, including faith in God, as a means to my own happiness. I married young, thinking that my husband's job was to love me and make me happy. And I dreamed of the day we would have a nice house, kids, and a secure future. Eventually, we had all of those things. The problem was, they didn't make me as happy or fulfilled as I thought they would.

When God opened my eyes to His love demonstrated at the Cross, I saw that He alone secures and fills me. I don't have to pursue happiness. He is it! And as I follow Him in love, He transforms me into His likeness. He makes me holy *and* whole. This is the good He promises us in Romans 8:28-29:

> *"And we know that God causes everything to work together for the good of those who love God and are called according to his purpose. For God knew his people in advance, and chose them to become*

> *like his Son, so that his Son would be the firstborn,*
> *with many brothers and sisters."*

The good God works in our lives from every circumstance is our transformation into Jesus' likeness. We become brothers and sisters who look like Him. This process of making us holy is called sanctification, and it's a supernatural work—what God does for us. His good plan is to make us holy. But, He knows that true holiness results in true happiness. I'm not talking about self-righteousness, or religious practices, or legalism, but about the inner transformation He causes. He cuts away our sin nature little by little and fills us with His very own nature. We were made for this—true holiness—and it's the place of true happiness.

Unfortunately, this life is not always happy. But brilliantly, God uses the very pain and suffering that sin and evil cause to cut away the sin and evil inside our own hearts. It's as we experience the brokenness of life on earth that God reveals our *own* brokenness, and our need for Him. He reveals His glorious offer of salvation through Jesus Christ. He reveals things about Himself that we can only know in times of trouble, heartache, struggle, or loss. And He produces in us the maturity and holiness we are meant for as His children.

> *"Dear brothers and sisters, whenever trouble comes*
> *your way, let it be an opportunity for joy. For*
> *when your faith is tested, your endurance has a*
> *chance to grow. So let it grow, for when your*
> *endurance is fully developed, you will be strong in*
> *character and ready for anything."*

> James 1:2-4

Let trouble be an opportunity for joy? Was James crazy? If he was, so was Paul:

> *"We can rejoice, too, when we run into problems and trials, for we know that they are good for us—they help us learn to endure. And endurance develops strength of character in us, and character strengthens our confident expectation of salvation."*

> Romans 5:3-4

How can we rejoice in our troubles? Only by seeing God's sovereignty over our lives—His power that causes everything to work together for our good. Our good is to be made like Him in every way. When being made like Christ becomes our ultimate desire and dream, we begin to see our troubles for the treasure they really are: tools that accomplish that dream.

In the weeks before the accident, God spoke to me in His Word about His sovereignty over all things. Looking back over my journal from that time, I was floored by what He showed me and how I responded in light of what was coming. Here are a few entries:

2/4/2008

Genesis 42—"Everything is going against me!"— Jacob, v. 36

Some things are beyond our ability to understand. The scope of events is too big, or the time frame is beyond what we'll put up with. The intertwining of lives and circumstances don't make sense from where we sit. So God doesn't show us things ahead of time that we can't handle or receive. When they come, we say, like Jacob, "Everything is going against me!" He couldn't see God's hand in losing Joseph, in Simeon being jailed in Egypt, or in being forced to let Benjamin go to Egypt. But these events accomplished amazing things…If God had revealed to Jacob everything he, Joseph, and the rest of his family would have to go through to accomplish His good plan, Jacob probably wouldn't have cooperated. Sometimes we can only handle understanding God's plan when it's complete and has accomplished the good that God intends. Sometimes we can't handle it at all.

Lord, help me to know and understand everything I possibly can about You, Your plan and Your Kingdom. Thank You for all You have revealed about the past, the present, and even the future. Please help me to trust You when things happen that I don't understand. When "everything is going against me," remind me that You are in control of it all. Help me to trust that You are working all things according to Your plan for our good.

I wrote those words exactly one week before Lauren's accident. Did I lean on what they taught me about God's goodness and control as I got the news that my daughter had gone to heaven? No. I didn't even remember they were in my journal until I got it out three years later to write this chapter. But the truths God planted in my heart that week were the seeds of what He would grow in me over the next year.

2/9/2008

Genesis 47-48—Joseph saves his family

Matthew 26—Jesus arrested

Both of these stories are full of two things: man's choices (mostly sinful), and God fulfilling His plan. Great good accomplished <u>through</u> the choices, even evil choices, of sinful men. God knew we would need pictures of this enormous truth. And even in these examples, where we can see the whole picture including the end result, we have a hard time comprehending it all. How much harder, then, must it be to comprehend the sovereignty of God in my own life in the <u>middle</u> of the story? From my perspective, I can't even begin to see how the bad things in my life could possibly be part of God's plan. But they are. I don't know if He ordained them, but He ordained to use them.

2/11/2008

(The day of the accident, before it happened)

Psalm 28:1—"Please help me; don't refuse to answer me. For if You are silent, I might as well give up and die."

Let me just say that I was speechless when I read this verse I wrote in my journal just hours before the accident. I found it almost three year later, realizing only then what I couldn't see that day. God had shown me in Scripture the prayer I would instinctively pray out of the depths of the most excruciating anguish and fear I would ever experience. I didn't remember writing these words, but my heart desperately whispered them just hours later, and I continued to pray them for months. I truly wanted to give up and die, knowing that if God didn't answer my cries, I just might. But oh, how He answered!

Back to God's sovereignty, I wrote the day before the accident about the Jewish leaders who accused Jesus at His trial. Jesus remained silent; He wouldn't answer their questions. What I saw there was that Jesus doesn't answer to His creation—not to them and not to me. Even though God welcomes our questions, we must be careful not to demand answers, thinking God *owes* us an explanation. On the morning of the 11th, I saw a contrast to this in the prayer of Psalm 28, a humility in the way the psalmist cried out to God. My prayer that day was:

> *Lord, I want to approach You in humility, understanding that You are the blessed controller of all things. You made and purchased me. You know me. And You know what every day of my life will bring. I trust You today Lord.*

Did I remember this prayer eight hours later when the policewoman at the accident scene told me Lauren had died? Shamefully, no. My husband never stopped trusting God's goodness, but I did. For the next year, I struggled to understand how God could love me and let something like this happen to me.

Before the accident, I understood God's love and sovereignty *in theory*. But when tragedy struck, suddenly God's sovereignty seemed at complete odds with His love for me. Knowing God could use bad things in His perfect plan didn't *feel* loving when something bad actually happened. I tried to respond with trust in this God whose love now seemed so foreign to me. But it became more and more apparent that I couldn't, even as I sought Him for the hope I desperately needed.

Truth be told, deep inside I felt betrayed by God. I was afraid at first to admit this to myself, but eventually I couldn't ignore it. I battled for a year with questions like, "If God truly loves me and is all-powerful, how could He hurt me so much?" My trust in Him was badly damaged. He had awakened me to His love, I drew close to Him for seven years, and then He wounded me. It felt like a fatal blow. How could I ever again trust the goodness of God if this was His will? And worse, if I did trust Him again, would He hurt me again?

February 9, 2009 fell on a Monday—one year after the Monday of February 11, 2008, the day Lauren went Home to heaven. It was a day of confrontation in my heart. God had poured out His love on me in an experiential and life-giving way for years before the accident. Days before, He taught me that He is sovereign over all things. Yet here, a year later, I still couldn't reconcile the two in my heart or my mind. And it was tearing me apart. Passages of scripture like Psalm 91 still often confused and angered me.

"This I declare of the LORD:
He alone is my refuge, my place of safety;
He is my God, and I am trusting Him.
For He will rescue you from every trap
And protect you from the fatal plague.
He will shield you with His wings.
He will shelter you with His feathers.
His faithful promises are your armor and protection
Do not be afraid of …
The disaster that strikes at midday."
Psalm 91:2-5a, 6b

The Holy Spirit had faithfully shown me the full picture of what Lauren experienced the day of the accident, but I still struggled with the psalmist's words. Lauren's physical body hadn't been protected that day, and neither had my heart. The horrific pain I now lived with daily caused me to ask, "How could this apply to me or my daughter anymore?" My heart would rail against this promise and others like it: *God didn't protect my daughter!* This is how I felt, even though I knew He *had* protected her through salvation and she now lived with Him.

Up to this point, I refused any words or scriptures of comfort from God or others. All I wanted were assurances of His promise that Lauren and I would be together again one day. That was the only comfort I thought I needed. So, even though Jesus was clearly present with me through His Word and His church during that first year, inside I held Him at arms' length. I didn't really trust Him. After all, it was actually me I thought God hadn't protected.

This was my mindset on the morning of February 9, 2009, and I wanted to overcome it, to be able to drop my arms and let Jesus pull me into His embrace. I knew I was fighting Him for answers that wouldn't ease the pain of grief even if He chose to give them to me. I realized what I needed was for Jesus just to hold me.

2/9/2009

Pull me into Your lap and wrap Your arms of love around me. Soothe the pain and quiet my fear. Fill me with faith—I'm so poor, so lacking, so weak. I know now that You've been calling me to You for this reason, while all I could do was beg You to give me my life back, my way, or just to take me home. I haven't wanted to accept my life the way it is now. I can't, until I let You hold me and comfort me. I haven't surrendered to You, not really. I've fought and fought, while You just wait for me to give up. Lord, it's so hard; I don't want to accept Your Sovereignty, Your plan. But fighting You gets me nowhere, and leaves me with a really banged-up faith. I must let go, surrender. You are God. I am not.

I knew I was still resisting, because I didn't really trust the heart of God toward me. I mentally acknowledged that He was sovereign and all-knowing. He sees the end of the story, and has even told us what it is: all will be restored because of what Jesus did. I knew I would be with Lauren again and the pain would be gone forever. But I was getting hung up on this thought: *Since God knows the happy ending and so do I, does He discount my present pain and want me just to "get over it?"* After all, that's how I was trying to deal with grief. So, it's what I imagined God was doing, too.

I was stuck. But God wasn't. I felt a strong urge to bow before Him. I needed to physically acknowledge that He is sovereign and that I was ready to surrender fully to Him. I ended up flat on the floor, declaring every reason I could think of that made Him rightfully the Lord of all. "You are the Creator, Sustainer and Provider of all things. You have redeemed all of fallen creation from sin and death. You humbled Yourself in willing surrender to the Father's plan, becoming a servant. You died the most painful death for Your lost children. You reign now in majesty and glory, putting all things under You. You have victory over all enemies, even the greatest one—death." And then the hardest question confronted me again: "How can God be sovereign in all things, even painful things, and still be loving and good in all things?" I couldn't see past my constant pain to His goodness and love for me.

But then, God gave my mind a picture: I'm holding my infant child while the doctor gives her an immunization; I comfort her, but don't stop the doctor. I remembered doing just that. I intentionally took each of my children to the doctor to receive shots. Why? Because I knew that even though they were painful, they were also necessary and good. *This knowledge, however, didn't keep me from hurting with my child or comforting her through the pain.* I hated to see my kids hurt, even when it was for a good reason.

I got up to record this picture along with the understanding that flooded my heart through it. As I did, I recalled a vivid memory of something that happened to Lauren when she was fourteen. She sliced her leg open in a superficial but long gash, and she needed stitches. So Scott and I took her to the emergency room. Before the nurse stitched her up, she gave Lauren several shots of topical anesthetic around the gash. Lauren cried and screamed, squeezing our hands in pain.

Scott and I both hurt for her, comforting her through our own tears. *But we didn't stop the nurse.* We knew what she was doing was good and necessary, that the pain was only temporary. She wasn't *harming* Lauren; she was *helping* her, even if it didn't feel like it. Did this knowledge keep us from feeling Lauren's pain? Did we tell her just to "get over it, it'll be done soon?" No! Our daughter was in pain, and that caused us pain. We wanted, and needed, to comfort her.

This is no less true of God, who is our loving Father. Yes, He's sovereign. Yes, He allows pain into our lives. And yes, He knows it's for good and only temporary. But, that doesn't mean He discounts our hurt in any way. He's not disconnected from it. In fact, the book of Hebrews teaches extensively that Jesus is our perfect High Priest, not only because He brings us to God through His sacrifice, but also because He became one of us. He understands us—all the joy and sorrow of being human—because He experienced it all Himself. We can never say that God doesn't understand our pain. Christ came to help us through it, and,

> *Therefore, it was necessary for Jesus to be in every respect like us, his brothers and sisters, so that he could be our **merciful** and faithful High Priest before God. He then could offer a sacrifice that would take away the sins of the people. Since he himself has gone through suffering and temptation, he is able to help us when we are being tempted.*

> Hebrews 2:17-18

Through His own suffering, Jesus came to know what it's like to be us in this broken and hurting world. He was tempted to give up on God's plan in the midst of His pain, just like we are, yet He didn't (see Matthew 26:36-46). He knew that His Father's plan was good. He trusted His Father's heart, even while enduring more suffering at the hands of evil than any of us ever will. No, we can't say that God doesn't understand our pain. The sorrows of God's children cause His perfect Father's heart to break when ours do. He sees into our hearts and longs to hold and comfort us in our pain. *"Praise be to the God and Father of our Lord Jesus Christ, the Father of compassion and the God of all comfort, who comforts us in all our troubles"* (2 Corinthians 1:3-4).

But this God of all comfort doesn't just see our hearts and commiserate with us. His comfort isn't powerless, empty words. It's much greater than that, because He's not only compassionate and loving, but *sovereign* as well. Yes, what I discovered was that God's greatest comfort in my suffering was the very sovereignty I resisted for so long. He is fully able to cause all things to work out for our good—as we trust Him. But we must choose to believe this even when those things don't feel good. He sees our hearts and suffers with us, and *at the same time,* He sees the entire story and rejoices over all He has accomplished. Pain isn't the end of the story; evil doesn't win. Because of this, we can experience joy even through our suffering. We can know that it accomplishes good and truly is only temporary. And we can trust that God will carry us and comfort us through it. He can see all these things; so can we, if we choose to have eyes of faith.

> *"For our light and momentary troubles are achieving for us an eternal glory that far outweighs them all. So we **fix our eyes** not on what is seen, but on what is unseen. For what is seen is temporary, but what is unseen is eternal."*
>
> 2 Corinthians 4:17-18 (NIV)

And, we can let God show us at least some of the good and necessary things our suffering accomplishes, in us and in others. He does it as we share with them His faithfulness, comfort and eternal hope.

> When you walked upon the earth
> You healed the broken, lost and hurt
> I know you hate to see me cry
> One day you will set all things right.[19]
>
> —"Your Hands," J.J. Heller

---

[19]   J.J. Heller, "Your Hands," (Stone Table Records, 2009).

Chapter 8—Good from Tragedy

Seeing good come from tragedy can be a tricky thing. Before I experienced tragedy personally, I thought I understood it. From an eternal perspective, temporary suffering, loss or struggle seemed endurable and even acceptable if it produced eternal good. The trade-off made sense.

I could understand it like this: touching something hot produces pain, but it's pain that we need, to keep us from greater harm. In the same way, pain in this life points to something that's wrong here—we're separated from God. Would it be merciful of God to remove all the consequences of my sinful choices, only to let me die in my sins and experience eternal punishment apart from Him? Would it be loving for Him to remove the brokenness sin brings, so that I never realize my need for His salvation? God allows consequences and brokenness to touch us in this life to keep us from eternal harm. We live with the personal consequences of our own choices and the general consequences of universal evil. All of it is meant to show what destroys us and point to the One who can save us.

Since 2001, desire to know God and be with Him forever had helped me gain eternal perspective. But because it was only hypothetical, I lost touch with the very real heartache that suffering causes here on earth. So when the truth moved from theory to reality in my life, my understanding and acceptance of it crashed and burned.

6/19/2008

I've always believed that it's right and good for God to prioritize the eternal over the temporal. And if I do too, I should understand and accept earthly trouble for what it will accomplish eternally. I know that's all still true, but I can't feel it right now. My pain seems to say more and more, "How could God expect me to endure this if He really loved me? Why does He intervene every day to save others? How can He love me and let me suffer so?" (This was before God addressed my problem with His love and sovereignty.)

From the beginning, I was thankful to hear reports that people turned to Christ after Lauren's memorial service. I even had the joy of leading my own sister-in-law to faith in Jesus. And to this day, I can't imagine choosing (if I could) to have Lauren back here if it meant those people would never know Him. After all, the pain of my separation from Lauren is temporary. Their separation from God would be eternal.

But suddenly I found myself aching when people talked about the good things God was doing. One reason was because it felt like those things were supposed to make it all ok, and it wasn't. The trade-off no longer made sense. Was Lauren's life here less valuable than what God was doing in others? The second reason it hurt to see good from our tragedy was that I was the one paying for it.

6/15/2008

> *Lord, I don't want to be here anymore. It hurts too badly. Every day it seems to hurt worse. I guess the shock is wearing off. And there are so many things that stab the wound. Like today, I listened to a conversation about the spiritual growth of some of the students and how You are working in and through them. A large part of what's happening is because of what happened to Lauren. Why was I the one chosen to make the sacrifice for all the others? My daughter dies, and the others grow. Why was I the one to get the hard part? Why did I have to lose so much so others could gain? The pain is going to destroy me if You don't do something, Lord. Please.*

The Anchor

As I sat outside on the porch that day, crying over my journal, I heard the Holy Spirit very clearly: *Look at the Cross.*

So I did. And this is what I saw:

> *God Himself gave the greatest sacrifice ever made so His lost children could gain. He sacrificed His beloved Son so that we might gain eternal life instead of eternal death.*

God the Father—a parent—understood the pain of sacrifice for others' gain.

The Holy Spirit brought to mind a CD my friend Julie gave me called *When Life Hurts Most*. I've learned to pay attention to these kinds of promptings, so I found the CD. On it, Louie Giglio talks about our anchor of hope in times of trouble and suffering. What was that anchor? *The Cross.* Here, like so many times when I cried out to God, was His answer, repeated. I told someone once that whenever I begged God for help in my grief, He didn't just answer me one time. He backed up a dump truck and buried me in answers. Such love! He is so faithful.

The five points of Louie's message were: 1) At the cross, I see God loves me; 2) God allows freedom, but maintains control; 3) God can use the worst for eternal good; 4) God paints on a canvas bigger than we can see or understand; and 5) God understands—*He* sacrificed so *we* could gain.

> *Lord, You understand my sacrifice. Yours was the greatest ever made. You have never allowed me to experience anything that You didn't experience. Because of that, there's nothing You don't understand. Thank You for always turning me back around into Your arms. I love You. Thank You for loving me. Please hold on tight.*

I continued to speak to the Holy Spirit about these things over the next few days.

6/16/2008

> *Is God good? Does God love me? The answer to these questions is found only at the cross. At the cross, the obvious answer is YES!*

> *Paul says in Romans 8 that nothing can separate me from God's love. Nothing that comes in this life can change the fact that God loves me. But can I*

*be separated from receiving and knowing His love?
I think the answer to this is yes. The darkness of
tragedy and grief can make it hard, if not impossible,
to see God, at least for awhile. It can cause me to
stumble into doubt and fear. It can make me doubt
God's love. Tragedy can hide God's love from me, if
I keep my eyes focused on the circumstance. That's
why even, and especially, in my darkest hour I must
look at the cross. In this darkest of hours in my life, I
must return to the cross and see once again the glory
and power of Christ's love displayed in the most
terrible, yet beautiful, sacrifice for me.*

*Make me aware today, Lord Jesus, of Your love
displayed at the cross. That love hasn't changed.
Help me to see it again…*

Three days later, I asked God to reassure me of His love.
I hated being so weak, but that's where I was, and that's
where He met me. The same day, I received an email from
our worship pastor with a song file in it. It was a song he
asked me to sing, called "At the Cross."

> At the cross I bow my knee
> Where Your blood was shed for me
> There's no greater love than this.
> You have overcome the grave
> Your glory fills the highest place
> What can separate me now?[20]
> —"At the Cross," Darlene Zschech
> and Reuben Morgan

---

[20] Darlene Zschech and Reuben Morgan, "At the Cross" (Hillsong
Publishing, 2006). Used by permission.

Once again, Jesus, You point me to the cross. You really did die for me, and You would have even if I were the only one. What can separate me from that kind of love?

Thank You Father, for the good You brought from Your own tragedy. Thank You for all we gain because of Your sacrifice. Keep me anchored in Your love at the Cross.

The Megaphone

The message I listened to about the Cross had a second part—"The Megaphone of Hope." In it, Louis Giglio says that the suffering of the cross is a megaphone of hope to the world. Jesus spoke to His Father about the cross: *"Glorify your Son so He can give glory back to You"* (John 17:1). The cross was His glory and the glory He gave His Father. How? With it, He put the love of God on brilliant display. He destroyed the power of sin. He overcame death.

Our suffering can also broadcast the message of hope to the world.

"I waited patiently for the Lord to help me,
and he turned to me and heard my cry.
He lifted me out of the pit of despair,
out of the mud and the mire.
He set my feet on solid ground
and steadied me as I walked along.
He has given me a new song to sing,
a hymn of praise to our God.
Many will see what he has done and be astounded.
They will put their trust in the Lord."
Psalm 40:1-3

When God shows up to carry us through something that would otherwise destroy us, people notice. Suffering magnifies the message of my life more than anything, just like the cross magnified the heart of our Savior God. If I refuse to give up my faith in Christ's love and my hope in His resurrection, that tells people it's something worth believing. And if I pass through the valley of the shadow in the arms of my Comforter, His infinite worth is broadcast to a world that needs Him.

This is exactly what happened in the Thessalonians' lives as they suffered severe persecution. Because of their joy and perseverance, Paul told them,

> *"You yourselves became an example to all the Christians in Greece. And now the word of the Lord is ringing out from you to people everywhere, even beyond Greece, for **wherever we go we find people telling us about your faith in God**... And they speak of how you are looking forward to the coming of God's Son from heaven—Jesus, whom God raised from the dead. He is the one who has rescued us from the terrors of the coming judgment."*

I Thessalonians 1:7-8, 10

Beside this passage, I wrote in my Bible, *"It is my prayer that this will describe my life."* I've come to mean that with all my heart. I'm so thankful God gave me a message of hope that a hurting world will listen to because it's broadcast through the megaphone of personal suffering. I experienced this thankfulness for the first time in May of 2009.

Celebrate Recovery is an amazing ministry of healing in Jesus Christ for all who struggle with hurts, habits, and

171

hang-ups. It reaches the broken. Our church not only offers it on campus, but takes it into prisons as well. The Saturday before Mother's Day, 2009, several of us went with a CR team to Turley Women's Correctional Facility in north Tulsa. We served the ladies lunch and held a service with music and testimony. It was the most real and beautiful time of worship for me, because as I sat among those women who could no longer hide their brokenness, I realized I didn't have to hide mine.

After the service, we had a few minutes to visit with the women. I approached three of them sitting against a wall, introduced myself, and asked how I could pray for them. They were very guarded, and didn't respond at first. Finally, one of them said, "I miss my kids." The other two agreed, and said I could pray about that for them. Their faces masked the pain I was sure they felt, pain they thought I couldn't possibly understand. And before Lauren's accident, they would've been right.

I knew I could break down the wall between those precious hurting moms and myself. So I took a deep breath and told them about my daughter and how I hadn't seen her for fifteen months. Instantly their eyes mirrored the pain in my own, and they instinctively reached for me. The wall was gone. They knew I would pray for them as one who understood. As I walked away, I realized my suffering had made it possible for me to reach people I couldn't before. And I was thankful.

From the first day, God gave us many ways to minister to others through our suffering. I've talked about impromptu opportunities and about some of the impact Lauren's service had on people. Now I want to share some large-scale ways God has worked over the last three years.

The Lauren Michelle Crawley Mission Scholarship Fund

My parents lived in Houston at the time of the accident, so they didn't arrive until the next afternoon. They had time to talk with friends before heading to Tulsa, sharing the news and asking for prayer for our family. Within a day or so after my parents got to our house, Mom came to me and said that many of their friends wanted to show their love and support in a tangible way. They wanted to donate to a ministry in memory of Lauren.

After talking it over, we decided that what would express Lauren's heart, and the heart of our whole family, was to donate it to missions. But how? We sought the Lord, again looking to Lauren's life for direction. What we saw was a young lady who had a growing desire to take the Gospel to people who had never heard of the saving love of Jesus Christ. We saw her savings account dedicated to help fund her trip to Africa that summer. And God birthed the idea of a mission scholarship fund to help students take the kind of trips Lauren had wanted to.

Scott's brother Mike is a banker (another example of the many unique parts of the body of Christ God put to work for us). He helped us set up a bank account in time for Lauren's service to which people could donate. Friends, family, business associates, and prayer warriors we didn't even know, poured out the love of God on us by honoring the heart of our little girl—a heart to go wherever God asked her with the Gospel. Even Lauren was able to donate as we gave the money from her savings account. And so, the Lauren Michelle Crawley Memorial Youth Scholarship Fund was born.

Every year, students from our church apply for the scholarship to help them take mission trips around the world to share the Gospel. As of this writing, the fund has helped send more than 15 youth to Ghana, Nepal, and San Diego. One went this summer to Calgary with scholarship funds to minister to the homeless. And in 2010, God gave us an amazing new opportunity to use money from the fund to make a long-term investment in one church's mission to reach Ghana for Christ.

Lauren's Lighthouse Chapel

When Lauren was saving to go to Africa in 2008, the trip was planned for Kenya. But that spring, there was growing civil unrest there. So our youth pastor, Steve, made the decision to look for another ministry opportunity in Africa. A man in our church was involved with Maranatha Power Ministries (MPM) in Ghana. He introduced Steve to the founder of MPM, Apostle Francis Afotey Odai. (Apostle in this context is a title for one who spreads the Gospel of Jesus Christ and plants new churches.) They planned a trip for our youth that would include medical missions, nightly crusades, and street evangelism in the capital of Accra and many small villages. Students and adults alike were called upon to preach, share testimonies, teach Sunday School lessons, and speak on the radio. It was a God-ordained, Holy Spirit-powered trip.

While the group was there, MPM presented each member of the team with a personalized woven sash. During a worship service, Apostle Odai called them up to the platform one at a time to receive their sashes. Because Lauren was on the original list, he also called her name to present a sash to her. After a few seconds of surprised silence,

Steve came forward and explained why Lauren wasn't there. Almost without missing a beat, Apostle Odai exclaimed, "We will reach Ghana for Jesus and for Lauren!"

In March of 2010, Apostle Odai came to the U.S. and spent some time in Tulsa. Scott and I met him for breakfast one morning, where he told us of his dream to construct a church building for the people of Winneba, Ghana. Winneba is a fishing village on the coast west of Accra, where a young church was struggling to get established. Apostle felt that if they had a central place to meet, it would help. MPM had been able to purchase some land, but they needed funds to build the church. So he asked if we would be interested in donating money in memory of Lauren. We knew this was an opportunity from God to use the testimony of Lauren's life for growing His Kingdom. Through it, we could help realize her dream of taking the love of Jesus around the world. So we gave part of the money from the scholarship fund and part as our own gift. Building was to begin during a second mission trip our youth would take there that summer.

Our youngest son, Jonathan, was now old enough to go, so he applied to be on the team. I was asked to go as a sponsor. But after praying about it, I still had a heart for Russia, where I had been several times before. Later, that trip fell through, but I still didn't sense God calling me to Ghana. Even after we sent the money for the church building, I didn't consider going.

The trip was scheduled for mid-June. By late May, I was reading the book of Ezekiel in my personal quiet times. If you've ever read Ezekiel (this was my first time), you know he was a prophet of God who, by all human standards, was an utter failure. Not the kind of person today's world tells us to strive to be. He was called to warn God's wayward people to turn back to Him before He punished them. The people ignored Ezekiel, just like they had Isaiah and Jeremiah, and were eventually sent into captivity. So here was a man called by God to preach an unpopular message that the people rejected. But He was obedient and faithful anyway—the mark of true success in God's eyes.

Early on May 28th, I read Ezekiel 4. It's the account of God's first "object lesson" demonstrated through Ezekiel to the people of Israel. God commanded Ezekiel to do something very uncomfortable, painful in fact. He was to lie on his side—the same side without moving—for 390 days, eating only eight ounces of bread and drinking one jar of water a day. And he did it. (I won't tell you what he had to cook the bread with.)

5/28/2010, AM

> *Am I willing to sacrifice my comfort, my free time, my resources, to follow God's call to me? Or do I see God's will as something that will be easy and make me happy? Ironically, everything God calls me to do, even hard things, bring happiness and fulfillment—just not by worldly standards. Obeying and pleasing God, even to the point of giving up everything for Him, bring greater joy than anything in this world. They bring great reward and true happiness in the life to come, too.*

Right then, the Holy Spirit began a conversation with me about His plans:

> *Let me see every person and every opportunity You bring me, Lord. I don't want to miss You or Your*

> *plan for me because I'm feeling sorry for myself or because it's too hard. I want to show Your love to everyone You put in front of me, one person at a time. And if there are specific things You want me to be involved in this summer, please place them in my heart.*

With summer fast approaching, Jonathan was already committed to a number of camps and the trip to Ghana. I envisioned myself sitting around the house alone, falling into the pit of self-pity. It was a pit I hadn't moved far enough away from, and I still stumbled into it once in a while. So I asked God to show me where to get involved. I thought first of Vacation Bible School, a week of hanging out with kids that I always enjoy. Was that where God wanted me to plug in? I checked to see when it was scheduled and realized it was the week the youth were leaving for Ghana.

5/28/2010, PM

> *Somewhere in all this, I began to want to go to Ghana as part of the team. The thought and desire kept growing, so I asked God about it. I wondered if I should devote time to writing that week instead, but my thoughts of going to Ghana persisted. I asked God to take them out of my head if they were my own thoughts and not His. They grew instead.*

A big reason I didn't feel comfortable going to Ghana was my bad back. I have spinal arthritis and degenerative disc disease in my neck, so I worried about not being able to keep up or carry my weight. I knew the trip was physically taxing and I didn't want to slow the team down. Of course, I worried about my own discomfort too.

> *How would I make the long flight, carry luggage,*
> *or sleep? The Holy Spirit pointed me back to the*
> *passage I had just read in Ezekiel. God told him*
> *to do something very uncomfortable for 390 days!*
> *That throws out all my objections of discomfort*
> *and pain.*

But, I had another glaring objection: it was May 28th and the team was to leave on June 17th. If I decided right then to go, I would have exactly twenty days to make all the arrangements for an overseas trip. Would there be an open seat on the flights? How would I get my visa in time? What about immunizations?

But a surprising thing was happening in my heart. The more questions I had and the more I thought of all that had to be done, the more I was filled with peace. I could hear the Holy Spirit telling me, "I want you to go. I will provide everything you need." I've never felt a greater sense of certainty about something God asked me to do than when He called me to Ghana at the eleventh hour.

By noon, I had told my Bible Study group that meets on Fridays—that very day. It was the first time I voiced out loud my conviction that I was to go to Ghana. I felt silly even bringing it up. They would surely think I was irresponsible to try to take a trip like this without months of planning. But my sweet friends were excited and prayed for me then and there. That gave me encouragement to talk to Scott, who, I was certain, would think I was crazy. But he didn't even blink when I asked him if it was alright for me to go.

Next, I emailed Steve, our youth pastor and Ghana team leader. Again, logic told me he would say there was no way for me to go at this late hour. But instead, he replied, "I'll check with Apostle Odai. See if you can get a seat on the plane!" So I did. Of course, by now I knew there would be one, for every leg of the trip there and back. And there was.

The next two and a half weeks were a whirlwind of details that fell into place. My visa application came back in record time—a week and a half. I got five immunizations, shopped sales for skirts and shoes to wear everyday in Ghana, attended team meetings, planned children's activities, songs, and games, and prayed through a team prayer calendar covering every aspect of the trip. Then on June 17th, Jonathan, I and 27 other team members boarded a plane for Ghana, West Africa and the adventure of a lifetime.

I wish I could share with you everything God did during our ten-day trip. He was so faithful, powerful and present. But it wasn't because we were there. It was because *He* is there, always at work around His world. We were just privileged to take part in His Kingdom work in Ghana for a few life-changing days. He was faithful to give us strength despite little sleep, to help us offer God's love and salvation despite language barriers, and to join our hearts to Christian brothers and sisters we had only just met.

I saw for the first time, through the efforts we made, how God communicates His personal love and attention to people by meeting their physical needs. At our medical clinics, so many precious men, women, boys and girls discovered that God saw their need, and loved them enough to send help. I never understood before how much that demonstrates the love of God to someone who feels forgotten. I think the greatest truth the Holy Spirit taught me in Ghana was to reach out to one person at a time as He puts them before me. I learned not be overwhelmed by the vast sea of need in our world today. I can only meet one need at a time. In doing so, I show people that God sees them and that they are important to Him. If you remember, this was what the Holy Spirit taught me about God's purpose for His followers on the day He called me to Ghana.

One of the highlights of the trip for Jonathan and me was the day we went to see the site of the church being built in Winneba. Before the whole group saw it, Apostle Odai and a couple of men from our team took me there. Apostle shared his vision for a complex that would one day not only have a church, but a school and medical clinic as well. He paced off the land to show us how big it was. I spent time wandering the site and taking pictures so I could share it with Scott back home. One of our men, Gene, pointed out to me that the ocean was not far from the site. In fact, about a mile in the distance, we could see palm trees that lined the shore.

Our team, the construction crew, and the MPM youth team who came with us to Winneba, gathered later that day inside the stem walls of the new church for a dedication service. Beforehand, Steve mentioned how appropriate it was that the church site was near the coast, because not long after the accident, Scott and I chose the symbol of a lighthouse to describe Lauren's life. It seemed fitting, because of her many prayers for Jesus to shine through her and for the way she did just that, in life and death. So, we decided to name the church "Lauren's Lighthouse Chapel." At the dedication, we read Matthew 5:14-16:

> *"You are the light of the world—like a city on a mountain, glowing in the night for all to see. Don't hide your light under a basket! Instead, put it on a stand and let it shine for all. In the same*

> *way, let your good deeds shine out for all to see, so*
> *that everyone will praise your heavenly Father."*

Apostle spoke of the people who would worship within the very walls where we were standing that day. We sang, read more scriptures, and prayed for God to bless His church in Winneba. Scott was able to be at the dedication service by phone from his office thousands of miles away. When I returned with video and pictures, he told me they looked just like he had pictured.

Later I learned from Apostle Odai that MPM had only acquired the land after two other sites fell through. This site by the ocean was exactly where God wanted Lauren's Lighthouse Chapel to shine for His glory in Ghana.

Lauren's Lighthouse dedication service, July 2010

Lauren's Lighthouse, April 2011

Bracelets and Nets

Two of my friends, Phyllis and Katheryn, are very involved in ministry to the people of Ghana. After her second medical mission trip, Phyllis, a nurse, became burdened to find a way to help the poor with more than just a few days of medication. She had seen more cases of malaria than she ever wanted to, and prayed for a better way to fight this preventable and treatable disease which kills so many children. In September 2010, God gave her the answer. She and Katheryn started Kairos 10 Jewelry, a non-profit organization that employs Ghanaian women to make bracelets from African beads, giving them a sustainable income. Its purpose is to provide mosquito nets to the poor in Ghana. Each bracelet sold buys one mosquito net.

Phyllis returned in October from her first jewelry training trip to Ghana, bringing with her a beautiful purple beaded bracelet. She sat with me and told me the story behind it. It was her idea when she went to have a bracelet designed in memory of Lauren, whose place she filled on the first trip in 2008. Originally, Phyllis planned for the bracelet to be made with light blue beads, Lauren's March birthstone. But when she tried to explain this to the young woman named Believe, who made the first one, Believe didn't understand English well enough to get the idea. Instead, she became enamored with purple beads. Phyllis finally gave up and let Believe make the bracelet with purple beads, only to find out later that purple is the color of February's birthstone. February 11th is Lauren's heaven birthday.

After getting my permission to sell the purple bracelet as the "Lauren" bracelet, Kairos 10 Jewelry has produced and sold hundreds of them to those who know Lauren's story. The "Lauren" bracelet, along with many other beautiful designs, has helped Kairos "net" numerous villages in Ghana, preventing malaria among Africa's poorest.

Believe, Lauren bracelet designer, and me.

Residents at girls' home receive mosquito nets

For more information about Kairos 10, please go to their website: www.kairos10.com.

Audience of One

Scott received a call from God in 2003 to lead people to an awareness of God's presence in their lives through worship. Shortly after sensing this, our pastor asked him to serve as the interim worship leader for our church. Scott said he would pray about it, fully intending to say no. He felt unqualified to do it, and he told God that. "Lord, I can't do this." He heard God tell him, "You don't have to. I'm going to do it through you." And God did, for eighteen months.

During that time, the Holy Spirit taught Scott much about leading people to worship. He saw the importance of helping others recognize the presence of God and connect with Him through the words they were singing. And he realized that this happened best when he himself recognized God's presence and worshiped Him. Over time, these seeds of understanding grew into the concept for a worship ministry called, "Audience of One: A Concert of Prayer."

Scott began to pray that God would surround him with people who had the same vision as his for worship ministry. Over the next several years, He brought them to us. Scott's heart was for a ministry that would let him bring people before God to see His glory through creation and respond to His personal love for them.

After Lauren's accident, our hearts were lifted to the wonders of heaven and eternity spent with Christ. The more we shared with others what God was teaching us, the more we saw that this is our purpose on earth—to make God and His eternal plan in Jesus Christ known. As He was lifted up through our longing for heaven, Jesus was drawing others to Himself. A worship experience started taking shape in our minds that would lead people to see God in Creation, Grace, Eternity, and Purpose. It became our desire that through music, video, scripture, and personal testimony, people would encounter God the Creator. We wanted them to realize He is close and intimately involved in their lives. Our prayer was for them to then respond to His grace at the Cross, and have their eyes opened to eternity and to the eternal purpose God has for their lives here and now.

Lauren's life and our testimony of God's faithfulness to us through grief are a big part of Audience of One. So much of what God taught us and leads us to do for His Kingdom has come out of the eternal perspective Lauren's home-going gave us. Over time, we've even been able to see that, although Lauren's early departure from this life was not our plan, it was always God's plan. And what an amazing plan it is!

For more information about Audience of One: A Concert of Prayer, please visit our website: www.audienceofoneconcert.org.

Christmas Letter 2009

Although this letter was written before some of the events above occurred, it holds truths that God taught us about His plan while it unfolded. I wanted to share the letter last because everything God has done illustrates these truths.

Dear family and friends,

Merry Christmas! We are writing a Christmas letter this year for two reasons. First, we want to say a huge thank you to all of you for your prayers and support for our family. Sending Lauren home to heaven 22 months ago is the hardest thing we have ever done, yet God, in His mercy, has drawn us closer to Him and to each other. We know that a large part of that is due to your commitment to carry us in prayer to our Father. We will miss Lauren for the rest of our earthly lives, but we look forward with joyful anticipation to the day we will be reunited with her forever. We are so thankful that we don't have to wonder if she was "good enough" to go to heaven. She wasn't, just as none of us are. That is why Jesus came—to live a perfect life and to take the punishment for our sin so that we could live with Him forever. We have assurance that Lauren is in heaven today because she gave her heart to Christ for forgiveness and salvation, and she lived a life of faith in Him before her death.

Her life gave testimony to the eternal life she had already received from Him.

The second reason we are writing is to give honor and praise to our Lord Jesus Christ for His plan to turn our tragedy into a beautiful part of His love-filled work of rescuing people for the Kingdom of God. We are coming to understand that it has been His intention all along to use Lauren's home-going as a powerful tool for bringing others to Him. Isn't it just like God to take something Satan intended for *our* destruction and use it to destroy *him* instead?

Alicia has been able to share with groups of women, moms, and youth workers what God has taught her through Lauren's life here, and about her Home now. Jordan speaks of Lauren when he leads worship, connecting him to those he ministers to. Jonathan has grown in enormous ways as he has turned to Jesus to carry, strengthen and heal him daily. Scott speaks with people every day about the purpose of our lives in this world. And, his vision for a worship ministry is completely focused on revealing God through His creation, His grace in Jesus Christ, our eternal home, and our purpose in light of all that Christ has done. We know of several others who have been able to share Lauren's story with thousands of teens, impacting them with the importance of living lives of faith in Christ. (One is Zane Black, who told the "pink pearls" story at camp.) And, a scholarship fund established in her honor sends youth and young adults around the world with God's message of hope found in Jesus Christ.

All of these opportunities have come our way because of Lauren. They have been part of God's plan for her and for us since the beginning. Because it had become her life focus to make sure that people heard about the love of Jesus for them, we know that right now she is celebrating what God is doing through her. And He is even helping us see that His plan for all of us is far greater and far more beautiful than we could have ever imagined.

Our prayer this Christmas is that we will all be able to celebrate the beautiful yet difficult plan that God chose for Himself and His one and only Son, Jesus. It is a plan that began at His birth, but was formed in the heart of God before He created the world, to provide the Savior we all desperately need. May you receive the fullness of God's love for you in Jesus Christ this Christmas.

Thank you again for your many prayers, cards and thoughts for our family. To God be the glory forever.

The Scott Crawley Family

"For God so loved the world that He gave His One and Only Son, that whoever believes in Him will not perish but have eternal life."

John 3:16

"Then I saw a new heaven and a new earth...
God Himself will be with His people and be
their God. He will wipe every tear from their
eyes. There will be no more death or mourning
or crying or pain, for the old order of things has
passed away."

Revelation 21:1, 3-4

Dedicated to Lauren Michelle Crawley

We love you sweetheart. See you soon!

In 2001, I prayed "Lord, bless me indeed!" from the
prayer of Jabez. This prayer also asks God, "Enlarge my
territory." Looking back now over the ten years since I prayed
these words, I can see how God did exactly that, beyond
anything I could have imagined. A missions scholarship
fund sending kids around the world with the Gospel, a
church in Ghana, mosquito nets for poor African villagers,
and a worship ministry drawing others to our Creator, far
exceed any plans I could have made on my own. What a
beautiful way for God to bless our family! And one day it
will far outweigh our sorrow as we celebrate with Lauren
all He has done.

Chapter 9—Refined Faith

"These trials are only to test your faith, to show that it is strong and pure. It is being tested as fire tests and purifies gold—and your faith is far more precious to God than mere gold. So if your faith remains strong after being tried by fiery trials, it will bring you much praise and glory and honor on the day when Jesus Christ is revealed to the whole world."

1 Peter 1:7

2/24/2008

Trials come to prove my faith genuine. I've had a few trials in my life, but none that truly tested my faith. I've wondered what people think of my faith, because of the prosperity they see in my life. Good marriage, healthy kids, material wealth, etc. Were they thinking, as Satan did of Job: "Yes, Job fears God, but not without good reason! You have always protected him and his home and his property from harm. You have made him prosperous in everything he does. Look how rich He is! But take away everything he has, and he will surely curse you to your face!" (Job 1:9-11)

I, too, have wondered how strong my faith would be if it were severely tested. And I'm beginning to see that I've been pretty arrogant about it. I've judged others for not responding in faith, thinking them short-sighted. I haven't been very understanding of weak, human responses in times of trouble. Deep down, I considered questions, doubts, and lack of faith as earthly-minded.

Lord, forgive me! Teach me and change me. Carry me! I can now see my own blindness in making judgments. Lord, my faith is still there, but I feel like I'm just numbly going through the motions. It's like I'm on auto-pilot. Lord, I need you! Help me to search for You and find You (Jeremiah 29:13).

From the beginning, I realized that Lauren's home-going would be the greatest test my faith had ever endured. But it still surprised and dismayed me that I struggled so much. After all, I had a close relationship with Jesus. How could I doubt Him after knowing Him so well? Thankfully, He used what He always had—His Word and prayer—to draw me to Him and speak truth to my heart.

3/6/2008

"But you must remain faithful to the things you have been taught. You know they are true, for you know you can trust those who taught you. You have been taught the holy Scriptures from childhood, and they have given you the wisdom to receive the salvation that comes by trusting in Christ Jesus. All Scripture is inspired by God and is useful to teach us what is true and to make us realize what is wrong in our lives. It straightens us out and teaches us to do what is right. It is God's way of preparing us in every way, fully equipped for every good thing God wants us to do."

2 Timothy 3:14-17

"Without wavering, let us hold tightly to the hope we say we have, for God can be trusted to keep His promise…Do not throw away this confident trust in the Lord, no matter what happens."

Hebrews 10:23, 35

God has given me these words to encourage and admonish me to hold onto what I know. I can't throw out everything He's planted in my heart. When I'm tempted to jump ship, thinking to save myself from the agony of shaken faith, God commands me to stay in the boat, to "remain faithful to the things I've been taught," to "not throw away this confident trust in the Lord no matter what happens," and to "hold tightly to the hope I say I have, for <u>He can be trusted</u> to keep His promise." <u>Nothing</u> can change *that. He is faithful and will keep His promise. If I jump now to "save" myself, which is exactly what Satan wants me to do, I will perish instead. God can be trusted. I must stay with Him in the boat, even when I feel thrown around by the massive waves of circumstance. I'm safe with Him, and only with Him.*

Jesus, my only comfort, peace, and sanity is in You—Your character and Your promises. I don't know how I'll ever get through the rest of my life here. But I'm convinced that the only place for me to be is in the boat with You, clinging to You each day, one day at a time. Please Lord, when I'm tempted to jump ship, pull me away from the edge and hold me in your arms of love. You're my only peace in the midst of this storm, as turmoil rages inside of me. Calm my heart and mind, and help me to find peace and rest in You.

My commitment that day, to hold onto the truth of God's Word, proved to be the foundation from which the Holy Spirit counseled me through my grief. No matter how deep my pain went, the Truth went deeper. I clung to this by faith alone, no matter what I felt.

"I Believe"

3/13/2008

Faith in Christ, growing in my life for seven years now, has been the only anchor I've had over the last month since Lauren's physical death. For much of the time I've been sort of on autopilot, able to

*speak and live the truth, but not always feeling
secure in it. My emotions and thoughts have been
so chaotic that they aren't a good indication of
what's true. Over and over, I've had to stand on
what is true when I haven't felt it. The truth has
been—<u>God</u> has been—my Rock, my Refuge, my
Fortress, and I know He's the only reason I'm still
sane and functioning.*

In *Gone But Not Lost,* David Wiersbe penned words
that helped me continue fighting for my tenuous hold on
the truth:

> "Faith means clinging to God in spite of
> circumstances. It means following him when
> we cannot see, being faithful to him when we
> don't feel like it.
>
> Mourners need a creed; it is 'I believe!' We
> need to affirm this creed daily:

> I believe God's promises are true.
>
> I believe heaven is real.
>
> I believe I will see my child again.
>
> I believe God will see me through.
>
> I believe nothing can separate me from
> God's love.
>
> I believe God has work for me to do."[21]

These were truths God brought me back to time and
again. For a long time, I had to decide to believe them even

---

[21] David W. Wiersbe, *Gone But Not Lost* (Grand Rapids: Baker
Book House, 1992), 55.

though they often didn't feel true. Looking back now, I realize that I've *seen* four of these statements proved true: God's promises *are* true. God *did* see me through. Not even Lauren's home-going separated me from God's love. God *does* have work for me to do. The other two I know by rock-solid faith: Heaven *is* real. I *will* see Lauren again. But it was a long road through the fire to make it to this point.

Sifting

The Holy Spirit showed me very early in the journey that He values my faith greatly. Peter tells us that God values our faith more than gold. He wants it purified, proven and revealed to the world (see 1 Peter 1:6-7). God rejoices in this and so should I.

3/13/2008

More than anything, I want to please God with my faith (Hebrews 11:6) and receive the inheritance that Lauren's already received in part. I want to keep before me God's glorious promise to completely redeem all things in Christ Jesus… Lord Jesus, fix my eyes on You and all that You endured because of the joy set before You. Help me cling to You, knowing that You haven't and never will let go of me. I want so much for my faith to be proved genuine, knowing how much that pleases You and brings You glory. Lift my eyes above this trial of grief to the glory of Your promises—all I will inherit in You. I need You desperately today. My heart hurts. But through it all, I will cling to You, my only solace and comfort, peace and joy. I love You.

Though I'd had a close relationship with Christ, I didn't know how my faith would stand up when it was tested. After all, I could *see* the goodness of God in my circumstances. I had faith in Christ for salvation, but hadn't really needed it for daily life. Of course there were trying times. We had financial stress for several years early in our marriage. Scott is accident-prone and had three separate accidents: he fell off of a ladder onto his head; broke his arm, needing surgery and a metal plate; and had a screw put in his ankle after an accident on the beach. He also sustained third-degree burns in a flash fire at our house, requiring skin grafts on his hands and ankles. There were parenting challenges as well that discouraged me. But overall, my life was extremely blessed. So I wondered, *would I still have faith in God's goodness once I couldn't see it? How would I react to something bad?*

I discovered that only in severe testing is a whole new kind of faith born. How could I have faith that God would see me through until I had something to go through? How would I know that nothing can separate me from God's love if nothing ever tried? What good could I see God bring out of trials if I never experienced any? Would I ever have faith that pleased God if things were always in my control, if I never needed to trust Him for anything?

3/22/2008

Jesus never changes. And once I'm in relationship with Him, that never changes. Even in this horrible circumstance, He remains the same: faithful, loving, present and strong, my joy and peace. I've changed, and I confess I'm struggling with a faith I thought was stronger. I'm striving frantically to feel the solid, immovable foundation of Christ that I know is there.

7/1/2008

> *Lord, right now I live in the part of Your Kingdom where true reality is hard to perceive. I must live by faith rather than sight. It's so hard sometimes, especially since I have to see Lauren by faith now, after seventeen years of seeing her by sight. But You're teaching me, and I'm coming to understand: by putting me in a place where I must live by faith much more than ever before, You've positioned me to be able to please You. "So you see, it is impossible to please God without faith. Anyone who wants to come to Him must believe that there is a God and that He rewards those who sincerely seek Him" (Hebrews 11:6).*

Peter discovered this new kind of faith when he was severely tested. He lived for three years in close relationship with the Lord Jesus Christ. He received revelation from the Father about Jesus' true identity—*"You are the Messiah, the Son of the Living God"* (Matthew 16:16). Those were exciting times in Israel, and he was right in the middle of it all. Even when things came to a head with the religious leaders of the day and it looked like a battle was looming, Peter pledged, *"Lord, I am ready to go to prison with you, and even to die with you"* (Luke 22:33). He thought he had faith when everything was going his way, when he thought he was on the "winning side" and Jesus would become King of Israel. But Jesus knew differently.

> *"Simon, Simon, Satan has asked to have all of you, to sift you like wheat. But I have pleaded in prayer for you, Simon, that your faith should not*

*fail. So when you have repented and turned to me
again, strengthen and build up your brothers."*

Luke 22:31-32

The beauty of God's testing is that we can fail and still
grow stronger in faith.

3/22/2008

*God gives us examples throughout His Word of
ordinary people experiencing life just like I do
today. Their experiences are not pictures of perfect
faith, but of struggle, weakness and doubt. They
show us God's mercy, power and restoration.
Because the people that God called made mistakes,
lacked faith, and even rebelled deliberately, I can
relate to them. God can use their stories to teach me
about myself, a weak human being experiencing
life with Him. "The Lord is like a Father to His
children, tender and compassionate to those who
fear Him. For He understands how weak we are;
He knows we are only dust" (Psalm 103:13-14).
So I believe it's appropriate for me to look at Peter's
experience with fear and failure in a dark time, as
I try to deal with my own fear and failure during
the darkest days of my life.*

*My faith had never been severely tested. Therefore,
I didn't know whether or not it was strong and
genuine. Satan didn't either, because all he saw
was someone with great worldly blessing—someone
who had no reason to doubt or turn from God.
God allowed Satan to sift me like wheat, fully
intending to use this terrible loss to reveal His*

greatness, glory and strength. I believe Jesus is "pleading in prayer" for me, that my faith "should not fail." What I love about this account is that even though Peter did fail, Jesus received him back when he repented and turned back to Him. Not only that, but Jesus used Peter from that point on to strengthen his brothers and to take the Gospel to the world.

This shows me that even though I've failed, I can turn back to Him. I've doubted and questioned God, losing the eternal perspective He cultivated in me for years...I need to repent of my fear and unbelief and turn back to Jesus. His grace and mercy toward me is so great that He stayed with me even as I turned from Him. He answered my cries of pain and addressed my fears. He is the One who made me able to turn back to Him.

Lord, give me the faith to repent of my fear and unbelief. Help me to turn back to You, trusting You completely. May I be able to say, as Peter did, "These trials are only to test my faith, to show that it is strong and pure." And then will You use me to "strengthen and build up my brothers."

A Picture

As the Holy Spirit walked me through my fear and doubt, God fought the battle for my faith that I shared in chapter 6. He also taught me some of the purposes He has for our faith as we go through suffering. I saw one in Matthew 7, where Jesus gives a word picture of two different kinds of lives:

"Anyone who listens to my teaching and obeys me is wise, like a person who builds a house on solid rock. Though the rain comes in torrents and the floodwaters rise and the winds beat against that house, it won't collapse, because it is built on rock. But anyone who hears my teaching and ignores it is foolish, like a person who builds a house on sand. When the rains and floods come and the winds beat against that house, it will fall with a mighty crash."

Matthew 7:24-27

Two lives. One built by faithful obedience on the rock of God's Word. One built through disobedience on the sand of human wisdom. Both lives have storms—big ones. God doesn't keep the storms of life away from the obedient one. Yes, obedience keeps us out of a lot of trouble, but some kinds of trouble hit us all. Why does God allow this?

Because all of us—and this world—are broken by sin, resulting in life filled with struggle, pain and death. When we come to the Lord for salvation, we receive Christ's eternal protection—we will live with Him forever. Our spirits come alive; we are new creations, forever alive in Christ. In the meantime, we still live here in dying bodies and a sin-filled world. God's promise to us here is to carry us through this life, preserving our faith. He wants to use us for His work, and reward us in His eternal Kingdom. We aren't promised earthly protection from suffering. In fact, we are called to suffer as God's servants in this world: *"They encouraged [the believers] to continue in the faith, reminding them that they must enter into the Kingdom of God through many tribulations."* (Acts 14:22. See also Acts 9:16, and 1 Peter 1:6, 4:12-13.)

There is much written about why evil and suffering exist and how they relate to God. I won't debate the issue here. Instead, I want to focus on one thing that God accomplishes through the suffering of His people. When God's people go through suffering that is common to all, He gives those around us the very picture Jesus gave with His story of the two houses. When a devastating storm hits a believer whose life is built on the truth and promises of God, she may experience some topical damage, but her foundation remains strong and her life secure. She comes through the storm intact, sane, and ultimately stronger. That same storm destroys the life of someone who doesn't know God or obey the truth of His Word. At the very least, that person has no real hope. These two lives present a stark contrast easily recognized by those around us. And it puts a powerful truth on display: God alone is the sure foundation of life, and He deserves our trust. When He is faithful through our storms, it strengthens our faith and calls others to faith as well.

Just about anyone will say losing a child is the worst experience they could ever imagine; almost as devastating is losing a spouse, sibling or best friend. We've all seen losses like these destroy marriages, families, and lives. God, in defeating death and offering eternal life, is *the only hope* that can sustain us through the most devastating times in life. What better way to make this clear than to allow a tragedy common to all people to touch the life of a family established on the Rock of Jesus Christ? God knows His presence will carry them through. He knows He will sustain their faith when they can't. He knows He will give them healing and victory with His promises of reunion and eternal life. He knows that as that family clings to Him and refuses to let go, His infinite worth will be on brilliant display.

Who has the best opportunity to reach the lives of unbelievers: a person untouched by the common tragedies of life, or a person carried through those tragedies by God in an uncommon, even supernatural, way? From my experience, it's the second. The first has nothing to offer others. The second has faith in the unchanging God of the Universe to offer —the foundation upon which to build a life and weather every storm. And when that foundation is offered as a testimony to God's faithfulness, ministry is born.

Lord, Use Me

8/9/2008

"Remember how the Lord your God led you through the wilderness for forty years, humbling you and testing you to prove your character, and to find out whether or not you would really obey His commands."

Deuteronomy 8:2

God's testing of my character is important, because it reveals if I'm trustworthy enough to be part of His plan on this earth. Will I obey, love, seek, and serve Him no matter what? Or will I turn from Him, rejecting Him when life gets hard? Am I faithful? Do I trust Him? Can I be trusted with His message of hope and salvation, or will I stop believing the truth when things don't go my way? Am I working to fulfill my own plans or His plans?

Lauren's home-going reduced my life plan to one thing: try not to drown in grief. Yet it seemed that everywhere I turned, God gave me opportunities to minister to others— Lauren's friends, friends from my old neighborhood, Bible study members. At times, I resented this because I was so needy and broken myself. I felt empty, with nothing to offer. But God showed me how ministry would be a crucial part of my own survival and healing.

8/14/2008

"No one lights a lamp and then hides it or puts it under a basket. Instead, it is put on a lamp stand to give light to all who enter the room…If you are filled with light with no dark corners, then your whole life will be radiant as though a floodlight is shining on you."

Luke 11:33, 36

If I hide, God's light won't shine and darkness will have won. But being put into darkness gives me greater opportunity to shine into the darkness of other people's lives. I don't want to miss that opportunity…Lord Jesus, it's Your light that shines within me, and nothing can put it out. I praise You for that. I pray that You will help me not to hide Your light or refuse to let it shine on others.

Okay Lord, I think I hear You answering a question I asked yesterday: Why do people expect me to offer them comfort in their grief over Lauren? I'm grieving deeper than just about anyone. Yet people come to <u>me</u> for help. Just yesterday, my ex-sister-in-

law Holly asked me to help my nieces, Megan and Taylor. And my first thought was: I have nothing to give. It's all I can do to survive myself. But that's not true. I have everything to give—hope, peace, the truth, the Lord Jesus Christ. If I refuse to offer these things to Megan, Taylor, and Holly, I'm hiding under a basket the light Christ Jesus has put in me.

Lord, that's so tempting to do, because I'm in great pain. I've "earned the right," humanly speaking, to go off and hide, seeking whatever relief and healing I can find. My humanness says, "It will deplete you of any resources, time, and energy you have for your own healing if you reach out and minister to others. You deserve just to let others take care of you. You have nothing to give." But this is a lie from Satan. I'm discovering the truth of this from God's Word:

"The kind of fasting I want calls you to free those who are wrongly imprisoned and to stop oppressing those who work for you. Treat them fairly and give them what they earn. I want you to share your food with the hungry and to welcome the poor wanderers into your homes. Give clothes to those who need them, and <u>do not hide from relatives who need your help</u>. If you do these things, your salvation will come like the dawn. Yes, your <u>healing</u> will come quickly. Your godliness will lead you <u>forward</u>, and the glory of the Lord will protect you from behind…Feed the hungry and help those in trouble. Then <u>your light will shine out from the</u>

> *darkness,* and the darkness around you will be as
> bright as day."
>
> Isaiah 58:6-8, 10

The Holy Spirit reminded me of this passage because it speaks, like Luke 11, of light shining from us. He wants to use that light. Do you see it? He gave me a specific word about my family: *"Do not hide from relatives who need your help."* How like God! He wanted to use His light in my darkness to shine into the darkness of my nieces' grief.

> *Jesus, I am in awe of You. I'm humbled that You would bend down and speak to me so clearly. It wouldn't be any clearer if You visibly stood before me and spoke the words. I've heard You, Lord Jesus. Now empower me to obey...Give me the strength and compassion I need for this task. It is Your light that shines in me. It can never be put out. Help me not to hide it.*

That day, God showed me He uses our ministry to others to heal *us* as well. The very suffering He allowed me to experience became my point of service. His light of truth was to shine out of my darkness. If I would let it, my light would break forth into the surrounding darkness and my own healing would come quickly. I found this to be true. Every time I shared with others the hope I have in Christ, even in deepest grief, I was energized.

Two weeks later, I spent Labor Day weekend with Megan and Taylor and took the time to talk with each of them about Lauren, their relationship with Jesus, and their understanding of God's promises. They were both dealing with grief in their own way, and it gave me a better idea how to pray for them. I realized that letting God reach His lost or hurting children through me was the one thing I was passionate about. It gave me a desire still to live in this world.

"Yes, your healing will come quickly." God has been so faithful to walk with me every moment. He's revealed eternity to me, and given me opportunity and supernatural strength to minister to others. I can't explain it, but God is working through me, through my weakness, by being visible and strong. Each time I share what He is planting in my heart, each time I give Christ's hope to those who need it, He is glorified and I am brought a bit more back to life. It's amazing, but true: God's "cure" for the death blows of this life is ministry, by giving testimony to His faithfulness. And that's the fruit of refined faith in the life of His child.

> *"And they have defeated him (Satan) because of the blood of the Lamb and because of their testimony. And they were not afraid to die."*
>
> Revelation 12:11

The Call to Persevere

February 11, 2011 marked three years since Lauren was called Home. On that day, God called me to persevere in the faith I had fought for, the faith *He* had preserved and refined in the fires of testing. I was studying the life of Abraham—the part where he and Lot had to separate because of their wealth.

2/11/2011

Abraham had a promise from God that He would give Abraham's descendants all the land he could see (Genesis 12:7). Abraham was also Lot's elder. For these two reasons, he could have chosen the best land for himself right then. Why didn't he? Why did he let Lot choose first?

Because God had promised the land to Abraham's descendants and "Abraham believed God, so God declared him to be righteous" (Romans 4:3). He knew God would fulfill His promise in His way and time, even though it was much longer than Abraham expected. He didn't have a son for many years, long past child-bearing age. And when he finally did, God tested Abraham by asking him to sacrifice that son. But God was faithful through it all. Abraham struggled at times to leave the promise in God's hands. But through the greatest test of all—giving Isaac back to God—he "believed in the God who brings the dead back to life" (Romans 4:17).

Lot took the best land that day. But God blessed Abraham, giving him many descendants who eventually occupied the land. He brought the Messiah, Jesus, to all nations through Abraham's family. Now God's promises are for all who believe in Jesus Christ:

—He declares me righteous by my faith.
—He promises me a permanent home.
—He brings the dead back to life.

This is such an amazing lesson for the Holy Spirit to bring me today. It's been three years since Lauren went to heaven. I am more secure in God's promises than ever before, and I'm so thankful for that. Now here's this story of perseverance in faith. My life may seem like a long road. God has asked me to persevere for three years so far, but He asked Abraham to do so for much longer. And Abraham did, because he believed the ultimate—that his God could raise the dead.

And though Abraham believed God would give the land to his descendants, he knew his eternal home was far greater. "Abraham did this because he was confidently looking forward to a city with eternal foundations, a city designed and built by God" (Hebrews 11:10). That's why he could hold loosely to the things of this earth, letting Lot take the land God had promised Abraham's descendants.

Thank you, Lord Jesus, for this reminder to persevere in trusting Your promises. You made Lauren righteous because of her faith. You've made me righteous too. One day, like her, I'll be completely righteous as I stand before You. You've promised us a heavenly eternal homeland which You're preparing for us now. And You are the God who raises the dead. I will persevere in faith Lord, knowing that I'm getting closer and closer to the fulfillment of Your promises. I'll hold loosely to the things of this world, using whatever You entrust to me for Your Kingdom.

Chapter 10—Restored Intimacy

Many times on my grief journey I expressed frustration in my journals over not being able to feel God inside of me like I had in the past. Though I could see Him at work around me, the pain, turmoil and fear of grief were all I felt most of the time. As God sorted through the overwhelming emotions of grief inside of me, I prayed desperately that my intimacy with Jesus would be restored. I read in various grief books that the authors experienced new depths of intimacy with God because of their suffering. I wanted that too.

Nancy Guthrie, in her book *Holding on to Hope,* tells her story of the devastating loss of not one, but two children as infants. In a chapter simply titled "Intimacy", she writes,

> "It is uniquely through suffering that we can find our way to the very heart of God. In fact, there is no other pathway that can take us there.
>
> It is when we are hurting the most that we run to God. We recognize that we are powerless and that he is powerful. We pray and we see

him more clearly because we're desperately looking for him.

And in our looking for him, we find him to be more loving and faithful than we've ever seen him before. We discover an intimacy that we have never experienced before, perhaps because we're looking for him so intently...

Wouldn't you like to come home?

Rather than running from or resenting your suffering, would you be willing to look for God in it?

Would you allow suffering to lead you to the very heart of God, a place where you can find the comfort and peace that you crave as well as the hope that has the power to transform your tomorrows?

God wants to bring you to a place where you can say, 'I've not only heard of you, I've seen you! I know you!' (see Job 42:5). And perhaps he has used pain to bring you to that place. God wants to use the difficulties in your life not to punish you or hurt you but to draw you to himself.

Will you come?"[22]

How I longed to have intimacy with my Savior again! I knew if I could return to it, it would be deeper than ever before. How could it not? I was experiencing Him for the first time as my Comforter, my Counselor, and my Healer. I was seeing Him as my Sovereign Lord who controls every moment of life, yet holds me close through it all. My mind

---

[22]   Guthrie, 87-89.

perceived the reality of this, but my heart lagged behind. I needed a complete restoration of intimacy with Him. Working through my battles with fear and doubt and with His love and sovereignty made the way back clearer.

When the Holy Spirit finally silenced the lying voice of the Enemy that plagued me for eighteen months, my doubts were gone. My hope for the future was anchored in God's promises, and I was free to erase the distance I had kept from Him. But I didn't immediately run back into His arms. My faith was still fragile and tentative. Once again, the Holy Spirit, my amazing Counselor, led me back with the perfect wisdom of God's Word, and a personal call for me to respond.

Lay Your Head Upon His Chest

At the time, I was reading a book called *Abba's Child* by Brennan Manning. In it, he talks about the apostle John. John called himself the "disciple whom Jesus loved," not to set himself above anyone else, but to express that he understood his identity and worth were found completely in Jesus' love for him. Manning believes that John may have understood this for the first time in the Upper Room.

8/11/2009

"Now there was leaning on Jesus' bosom one of His disciples, whom Jesus loved…" (John 13:23). Today, we would say it more like this: "He laid his head on Jesus' shoulder" or "He laid his head on Jesus' chest" or "against Jesus' heart." It was an expression of intimacy between the two. By doing this, John revealed that he felt fully loved and fully safe drawing close to Jesus. He came to see

the love of Christ for him in a way that elicited a passionate and trusting response. It was in that embrace, against the heart of his Master, John found worth and meaning. It was the same for me. When the love of Jesus burst into my heart for the first time, it brought me healing and set me free. Knowing I'm loved by the Lord Jesus Christ gives me my identity and worth. When I'm fully confident in my Savior's love for me, I'm free to become all He made me to be. I want to be free and confident again in His love.

This morning as I sat down to read, my heart grew heavy when I realized that today marks eighteen months since I've seen Lauren. For comfort, I turned on my iPod and chose to play all of the songs instead of one playlist. I haven't done that in a very long time. This was the first song that played:

On God I rest my salvation
My fortress shall not be shaken…
I lay my head upon His chest
On God I rest.[23]

—"Psalm 62," Shane Barnard

Oh Jesus, I hear an invitation from You to me, such a sinner, doubter, and weak child. You're calling me to come and lay my head upon Your chest and to feel Your strong arms around me. You want me to know the healing power of Your tender love for me. Healing only comes here, in the

---

[23] Shane Barnard, "Psalm 62," (Waiting Room Records, 2007).

security of Your love. Draw me close today. Help me to rest securely in Your love, humbly knowing that I am one You love. It's here that I'm free, and I can love others graciously and generously. Let me rest in Your love today, to abide in You and You in me. I am Yours.

> *"Let all that I am wait quietly before God,*
> *For my hope is in Him…*
> *He is my refuge, a rock where no*
> *enemy can reach me.*
> *Oh my people, trust in Him at all times.*
> *Pour out your heart to Him,*
> *For God is our refuge."*
> *Psalm 62:5, 7b-8*

"Remain in me, and I will remain in you. For a branch cannot produce fruit if it is severed from the vine, and you cannot be fruitful unless you remain in me. Yes, I am the Vine; you are the branches. Those who remain in me, and I in them, will produce much fruit. For apart from me you can do nothing."

John 15:4-5

"Remain in Me." "God is my refuge." There is no life apart from God. He creates and sustains life. I only find true <u>life</u> when I draw close to Him and receive His true <u>love</u>. Without Him I'm lifeless, useless…When I remain in His love, I'm alive and bear fruit for His glory. It's in taking refuge in God as a weak and broken child (and sinner), that I am most fruitful.

> *Jesus, draw me close to Your heart. I come willingly into Your arms to lay my head against Your chest. How I need the healing power of Your love and presence with me!*
>
> *"I have loved you even as the Father has loved me. <u>Remain</u> in my love."*
>
> —*Jesus, John 15:9*

In response to the Holy Spirit's invitation, I felt myself taking tentative steps back into the arms of Jesus. But He didn't leave me to do it alone. He continued to speak to me, encouraging me with a picture of the tender love of my Savior.

8/18/2009

> *While reading a passage from a Bible study today, my eyes fell on this verse from Isaiah: "He will carry the lambs <u>close to his heart</u>" (40:11).*
>
> *This is the message God gave me last week. What tenderness and care my Shepherd gives me! When I was hurting and had no person to lean on, He was there just like He always is. He's used many people to comfort and carry me since the accident—partly, I think, because I couldn't feel Him close to me. He never left, but my pain was too great. It was all I could feel, so God cared for me through others.*
>
> *Gradually, I began to feel Him again within me. He set me free from fear and doubt. Then the wonder of His great love and heart of passion for me returned. When it did, He reached out,*

drawing me to Him on His own, not through any
person. I was ready to move into His arms and lay
my head upon His chest. I could feel His embrace
and hear His heartbeat. I had come home—a lost
and broken prodigal.

"So he returned home to his father. And while he
was still a long distance away, his father saw him
coming. Filled with love and compassion, he ran
to his son, embraced him, and kissed him."

Luke 15:20

For the first time in eighteen months, I felt close and
connected to Jesus. I knew my relationship with Him didn't
depend on my feelings, for He had certainly been present
and active the whole time. But I had missed the sense of
love, joy and intimacy that is a big part of faith in Him.
From this day on I continued to seek intimacy with Christ.
I came to know Him in ways that would have never been
possible without the journey I took through grief.

A Place No One Else Can Go

Most recently, I've come to experience, like never before,
God's *comforting* presence inside of me. Believers are taught
that the Holy Spirit lives in them, but do we understand
the reality of this truth? Before the accident, I knew God's
Spirit as the power that transforms me into the likeness of
Jesus and produces His fruit. Since the accident, He had
been the Counselor within me through my grief. But now I
was coming to a new realization.

There's a place inside each of us that we can't fully
express to anyone. It's that place no one can enter with us,

where we feel and experience things we can't describe. When I would begin to slide into the pain of a mother missing her daughter, or start to disconnect from life going on around me, I felt alone, unable to share it with anyone else. No one could really be "in there" with me. Gradually, the Holy Spirit led me to take those thoughts and feelings, as soon as they came, straight to Jesus. I found this helped me almost immediately. Then one day it hit me. The Spirit of Jesus lives *inside* me, *in* that place I can't describe to anyone, that place no one else can go. It was the place I felt all alone, but suddenly I saw that I wasn't alone, even there. And because He's there with me, I don't have to describe it to Him. He already knows! He feels my feelings and I'm not alone. What healing it brought to know this one simple thing. Throughout much of my grief journey, I thought that deep inner place was where I wasn't connected to anyone. But now I know better. Even there I'm never alone.

Just today, I read a story in Genesis that showed me there's a reason God meets us where no one else can. It's the story of Hagar. She was the servant of Abraham's wife Sarah, made to bear a son for Sarah and Abraham. After Hagar got pregnant, she began to treat Sarah with contempt. Sarah treated her badly in return, and Hagar finally ran away. Because of the choices of others and her own bad behavior, Hagar found herself pregnant and alone in the desert with no way to care for herself. And it was there that God revealed Himself to her in a most tender and intimate way.

The angel of the Lord came to her and told her, *"You are now pregnant and will give birth to a son. You are to name him Ishmael, for the Lord has heard about your misery"* (Genesis 16:11). Hagar's response is beautiful. *"Thereafter, Hagar referred to the Lord, who had spoken to her, as 'the God who sees me,' for she said, "I have seen the One who sees me!"*

(v. 13) She went back to Abraham, and there's no record of any more discord between her and Sarah. Could this be because Hagar's heart was at rest in the intimate love of the God who saw her in her time of desperate need, a time when she was all alone?

During her early years under the care of Abraham, Hagar most likely was unaware that God saw and provided for her needs. But when everything was stripped away, God revealed Himself to her personally. What joy it must have brought Hagar to discover that she was intimately known and cared for by God! This is something every one of us needs to know, and it most often takes a time of desperate aloneness for us to see *"the God who sees me."*

Hagar's story doesn't end there. Years later, after Isaac was born to Abraham and Sarah, Hagar's son Ishmael was caught making fun of Isaac. Sarah insisted that Abraham send Hagar and Ishmael away. Abraham was very upset by this, but God told him to send them away, and Abraham obeyed. At first glance, this seems cold and heartless of both God and Abraham. But taking a closer look, we can see otherwise. God promised Abraham that Ishmael would grow up to give him many descendants. I believe Abraham took this as God's promise to personally watch over and care for his son and Hagar.

And this is exactly what God did. Once again Hagar found herself in a desperate situation. She and her son were alone and dying in the desert, when the angel of the Lord appeared. He gave her God's promise to make a great nation from Ishmael's descendants. Then the angel showed her a well just as she and Ishmael were about to die from lack of water. From that day on, they lived in the desert under God's personal care.

Lord Jesus, it was during the most painful, desperate and seemingly hopeless times of my life that You revealed Yourself most tenderly to me. During a difficult time in my marriage, I felt alone, like my needs would never be met and I would never be able to change. You appeared to me then, in all the glory of Your love at the cross. Knowing You personally and receiving Your tender, passionate love changed both me and my marriage.

And when I was plunged into the pit of grief and despair, You came to me where no one else could. You saw me in my most desperate need. You never took Your eyes off of me, You never let go of me— and You told me that over and over. Oh how I love you Jesus!

Help me Lord, to draw close to You every day, even when things don't seem so desperate. For in truth I'm desperate for You every day, every moment. Help me to see and know that. Did Hagar know it when she returned to Abraham? Did she know and depend on You all the years she raised Ishmael in the desert? I want to know my need and draw close to You every day, no matter my circumstances.

Chapter 11—Renewed Vision

After nearly three years of counseling, I sensed that the Holy Spirit had healed the last of my grief wounds and set me on a path back into my Shepherd's arms. Then a strange thing happened. I found myself at a loss for how to relate to Him in the "ordinary-ness" of life. For over two and a half years, our times together in His Word, my journaling, and my prayers throughout the day largely centered on surviving the grief journey. Now I had made it to the other side of what I thought were all the issues, and I found a new one—how do I find meaning again in everyday life?

8/6/2010

> *I've dealt with the big issues of grief and now I'm left with the rest of my life to miss Lauren. I must somehow endure pain that will be with me from now on. How do I come to grips with that? And how do I live the rest of my life on earth with joy?*

My trust in the Lord was secure. A sense of awe and the wonder of His amazing love filled my heart again. I ran into His arms and experienced new intimacy with Him. But now, with His counsel about the deepest struggles of grief complete, I sometimes felt like I was left just to survive the days I had left on earth. I knew I needed daily interaction with God in order to find joy again. I knew I needed purpose.

God had faithfully used me to bring Him glory, often ministering to others as I struggled through grief. But it was most often *through* my brokenness and *in spite of* my apathy; it was rarely something I planned to do. Now, I needed a renewed vision of God's Kingdom purposes in this world. I wanted to be passionate about the work He still had for me to do. And I wanted to find joy in everyday life. I had to learn how to miss Lauren and still experience the fullness of God's plan for my remaining years on earth.

> *Everyone around me seems to be living on a different plane than I am—engaged, glad they are here, all their children healthy and growing. Though I find great joy and happiness with Scott and the boys, my heart is partially and firmly in heaven with Lauren, absent from here. In public, I act like I'm fully engaged, and I think people believe I'm fully whole. But on the inside, I struggle.*

I wasn't satisfied with just surviving the rest of my life, though it was a life I had come to terms with. So I continued to pursue daily relationship with Christ in His Word. I know He's the one who, through my dissatisfaction, kept faithfully drawing me to Him. As we met each day, the Holy Spirit addressed my need for joy and purpose by taking me back to something He taught me early in my grief journey.

True Reality in the Kingdom of God

In July of 2008, just five months after Lauren went home, the Holy Spirit opened my eyes to a fuller understanding of reality. I drew this in my journal:

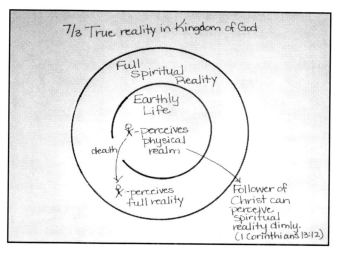

This diagram represents what God taught me about how a believer's life on earth relates to the Kingdom of God. Earthly life isn't far removed from His Kingdom; it's actually within it. Entrance into the full reality of God's Kingdom comes only through physical death.

7/3/2008

> *"Now we see things imperfectly as in a poor mirror,*
> *but then we will see everything with perfect clarity.*
> *All that I know now is partial and incomplete,*
> *but then I will know everything completely, just*
> *as God knows me now."*

1 Corinthians 13:12

I live within the Kingdom of God right now, much as a baby lives in the world before it's born. He's alive, but he's limited to the surroundings of the womb, and he can perceive only his immediate environment. When he's born, he moves past the womb into the greater realm of life that he already existed in but couldn't see or interact with.

I, too, have very limited access to the Kingdom of God. I live in this earthly part of it by sight and the rest of my senses. But there's a greater part I can't see, yet I can perceive it by faith. When Christ Jesus brought my spirit to life and placed His Spirit in me, He made me capable of knowing more than this limited physical world. I can see, recognize, and understand His Kingdom with eyes of faith. The more I let the Holy Spirit fill me, the more I can perceive and interact with God and His Kingdom.

I eagerly await my birth (through death) into the full reality of the Kingdom of God. But until that moment, I want to see it as clearly as I can by faith. I want to be able to participate in it through relationship with Jesus and in service to Him.

The spiritual realm of God's Kingdom is full of activity and participation in the work of redemption here on earth. Those who live in heaven today are at the hub of this activity. They're aware of, focused on, and, I believe, even involved in moving God's plan toward its completion.

Lord Jesus, what a beautiful picture!...Oh how I long to be born into the fullness of Your Kingdom! Until that day, grow me into the deepest understanding of it that I can possibly have from this side.

This was my continual prayer through the entire two and a half years of my grief journey. While the Holy Spirit counseled me through my struggles, I constantly pursued God's promises to His children. These promises led me straight to His eternal Kingdom. There I discovered that life in Christ is about so much more than earthly life, my own personal salvation or my future in heaven. It's about the glory of God and His Kingdom. It's about making Him known and worshiped among all people. My expanded vision laid the ground-work for God to lead me forward out of grief. As that journey ended, a new one began. Or maybe it's all been part of the same journey, the one God prepared for me long ago.

In January 2011, my pastor Hess Hester preached a series of messages about finding life in the Kingdom of God. I wrote this in my notes:

> *Knowledge of the Kingdom is not meant to lead us to ignore the world. We are called to make the world more and more like the Kingdom of God. Our gospel has grown too small. It's not about me and a "self-help" Savior. It's about the King, and bringing His Kingdom to earth.*

I believe a large part of God's purpose behind letting Lauren come Home was to lift our eyes to eternity, so that He could expand our vision of His Kingdom and our role in it now. The more I see God's Kingdom, the more I see the brokenness of this world. I see God's heart for those who need to be reached and brought into the Kingdom. It's the heart of a rescuer. And I find my heart opening in a new way to the lost and broken— the captives who need Christ's love to set them free.

A New Vision of the King

An unexpected result of my focus on the Kingdom of God came three years after Lauren went Home. One day, with my new Kingdom eyes, I saw its King as never before, and I fell in love all over again. On the third anniversary of Lauren's memorial service I wrote:

2/14/2011

I feel like I did almost ten years ago when Jesus first revealed Himself to me through the Cross. Back then, I saw for the first time the beauty and love of His heart toward me personally, and I was undone. Captured. In love.

Now He's revealing Himself to me as the Beloved King of heaven. All authority, power, majesty, honor, praise, and strength are His. He is exalted and worshiped by all there, every heart riveted to Him, every desire for Him. He is King above all. He doesn't have to take this place. It's just His. And His heart is filled with tenderness, humility, and self-less love. Oh, how I love Him! Once again undone. Jesus! You don't demand worship—it's just Yours. You don't claim all authority. You just are. Beloved King of all Kings, You became the Lamb. I cannot comprehend.

Over the course of several days, the Holy Spirit continued to speak to me about the wonder and majesty of Jesus my King. I saw Him in a whole new way. Consider these passages:

"Though he was God, he did not demand and cling to his rights as God. He made himself nothing; he

*took the humble position of a slave and appeared
in human form. And in human form he obediently
humbled himself even further by dying a criminal's
death on a cross. Because of this, God raised him up
to the heights of heaven and gave him a name that is
above every other name, so that at the name of Jesus
every knee will bow, in heaven and on earth and
under the earth, and every tongue will confess that
Jesus Christ is Lord, to the glory of God the Father."*

Philippians 2:6-11

*"In the beginning the Word already existed. He was
with God, and he was God. He was in the beginning
with God. He created everything there is. Nothing
exists that he didn't make. Life itself was in him,
and this life gives light to everyone. The light shines
through the darkness, and the darkness can never
extinguish it...But although the world was made
through him, the world didn't recognize him when
he came. Even in his own land and among his own
people, he was not accepted. But to all who believed
him and accepted him, he gave the right to become
children of God...So the Word became human and
lived here on earth among us. He was full of unfailing
love and faithfulness. And we have seen his glory, the
glory of the only Son of the Father."*

John 1:1-5, 10-12, 14

As I pored over these words, the Holy Spirit showed me
a pattern—the majesty of Christ Jesus the King *who became
the Lamb* slain for us. I saw it again and again:

227

*"**Christ is the visible image of the invisible God**. He existed before God made anything at all and is supreme over all creation. Christ is the one through whom God created everything in heaven and earth. He made the things we can see and the things we can't see—kings, kingdoms, rulers, and authorities. Everything has been created through him and for him. He existed before everything else began, and he holds all creation together. Christ is the head of the church, which is his body. He is the first of all who will rise from the dead, so he is first in everything. For God in all his fullness was pleased to live in Christ, and by him God reconciled everything to himself. He made peace with everything in heaven and on earth **by means of his blood on the cross.**"*

Colossians 1:15-22

*"In these final days, [God] has spoken to us through His Son. God promised everything to the Son as an inheritance, and through the Son he made the universe and everything in it. **The Son reflects God's own glory**, and everything about him represents God exactly. He sustains the universe by the mighty power of His command. After **He died to cleanse us from the stain of sin,** He sat down in the place of honor at the right hand of the majestic God of heaven."*

Hebrews 1:2-3

"Then I (John) wept because no one could be found who was worthy to open the scroll and read it.

228

*But one of the twenty-four elders said to me, 'Stop
weeping! Look, the Lion of the tribe of Judah,* **the
heir to David's throne** *has conquered. He is
worthy to open the scroll and break its seven seals.'
I looked and I saw a Lamb that had been killed
but was now standing between the throne and the
four living beings…'* **The Lamb is worthy—the
Lamb who was killed.** *He is worthy to receive
power and riches and wisdom and strength and
honor and glory and blessing.'"*

Revelation 5:4-6, 12

I read each passage, and I sensed the authors trying to
put their inspired thoughts into words. They somehow had
to describe the majesty of Jesus—King of kings *and* the One
who died for us—using the words of a language that was as
inadequate as mine. A human language. My mind sees far
less than they did with their eyes, and *I* can't find words.
How they must have longed for words they didn't have.

2/14/2011

*My heart feels things I can't express. My mind
sees Jesus, King of all heaven and earth and I
can't describe Him. The authority, power, and
command that are inherently His make me desire
Him so much. This holy desire to worship the One
true King—Jesus Christ, Son of the Father, Lamb
who was slain—is what my heart was created to
hold and to feel and to give Him alone.*

*I was made for You, Lord Jesus. I am only alive
when I see You, only complete when I worship*

> *You. And You live in me...Fill me, encompass me,*
> *bring me alive for You.*

This is a King worth serving, One worth living and even dying for. He served us in the most humble of ways. How can I not love and serve Him? He is the ultimate Rescuer—He rescued me. How can I not answer His call? In light of His majesty, authority, humility and love, the world and its cheap pleasures fade away. No wonder Paul could say,

> *"Yes, everything else is worthless when compared*
> *with the priceless gain of knowing Christ Jesus my*
> *Lord. I have discarded everything else, counting*
> *it all as garbage, so that I may have Christ and*
> *become one with him."*

> Philippians 3:8-9a

And,

> *"As for me, God forbid that I should boast about*
> *anything except the cross of our Lord Jesus Christ.*
> *Because of that cross, my interest in this world*
> *died long ago, and the world's interest in me is*
> *also long dead."*

> Galatians 6:14

"Why do you call me Lord?"

To be true servants of our King, we must see Him as He is—the supreme and most desirable Lord of all, who gave Himself for us. To see Him as anything less is to be that much less surrendered to Him in obedience to His call.

2/18/2011

"I saw a throne in heaven and someone sitting on it! The one sitting on the throne was as brilliant as gemstones—jasper, and carnelian. And the glow of an emerald circled his throne like a rainbow... Whenever the living beings give glory and honor and thanks to the one sitting on the throne, the one who lives forever and ever, the twenty-four elders fall down and worship the one who lives forever and ever. And they lay their crowns before the throne and say, 'You are worthy, O Lord our God, to receive glory and honor and power. For you created everything, and it is for your pleasure that they exist and were created.'"

Revelation 4:2b-3, 9-11

Lord, we don't really have any idea, do we? We use the term 'Lord' so lightly, often disconnecting it from the authority You have over our lives. You have a lot to say about that.

"So why do you call me 'Lord,' when you won't obey me?"

Jesus, Luke 6:46

"Not all people who sound religious are really godly. They may refer to me as 'Lord,' but they still won't enter the Kingdom of Heaven. The decisive issue is whether they obey my Father in Heaven."

Jesus, Matthew 7:21

> *I don't want to call Jesus 'Lord' without meaning He is my authority whom I will obey. I want to commit to obedience every day, exalting You, Lord Jesus, as my Master and King. I will serve You with gladness in the power of Your Holy Spirit given to me by Your grace. I love You—lead me today. Help me to see You.*

Here was the call from my Lord and King, the One who died for me, the One I had fallen for completely. To live my love for him in obedient service would be the joy of the rest of my life on earth. I am far from perfect in obedience, but I'm learning that my King is so tender and willing to walk me through each day with love and patience. And He's teaching me that there is much to be done for His rescue mission. As one He has rescued, God is calling me to become a rescuer.

Looking back at my journals, I found several entries in which God spoke to me two years earlier about rescue.

2/15/09

> *The Lord has rescued me; I'm eternally safe in Him. He's re-establishing my faith in His great love for me, planting me firmly in His mercy and grace. I'm held tightly in His grip. As He does this, I sense now that He is saying, "You are secure, rescued. Nothing can snatch you away from me. Now, it's time to begin rescuing others."*

> *Has what I've been through made it possible for me to get closer to those God wants to rescue through me? Will they trust me more, knowing that I was rescued too? Lord, show me what to do. Use me. I am Yours.*

At the time, I wasn't sure what God wanted me to do in response. But I realize now that He gave me opportunities all along the way—many of which I described in chapter eight. And He continues to give more. By calling me to His rescue mission on earth, God is demanding greater obedience from me than I've ever had to give. At times, it scares me. I have to fight the urge not to surrender, because the task is so daunting. But then I remember the lesson I learned in Ghana: take God's love to one person at a time. That's the work of the Kingdom. That is obedience to my King.

The Forgotten "Trokosi"

On my second trip to Ghana in 2011, our team visited the Girls' Vocational Training Center in Frankadua. It's a ministry that rescues teenage girls from slavery to fetish priests. The girls are given to the priests by their families as payment, or "guilt offerings," for alleged offenses against the gods. They are called simply "Trokosi"—wife of the gods. They are stripped of their identity and all self-worth, and made to serve in the fields and as sex slaves to the priests.

When their time of servitude is over (for some, this is never), or they find a way to escape, they are often scorned by their tribes and rejected by their own families. This is because they are feared for their connection to the priests and gods, or because they have dishonored the gods.

The Frankadua Training Center has been able, with funds provided by the Ghana Baptist Convention, to purchase girls from the priests. The girls are taken to the training center to live for three years, during which they study English, mathematics, and business. They're taught a trade such as hairdressing, catering, or sewing. Most importantly, they receive counseling and hear the Good

News that Jesus loves them and came to rescue them from the destruction of a sinful world.

After completing three years of training, many girls have put their faith in Christ and started down the road to healing. The center then gives them "seed" money to relocate, obtain housing, and begin their businesses. Though it's hard for the training center to keep up with all of the graduates, they've been able to stay in contact with enough girls to know that the program is successful. To date, over 300 girls have completed the program.

Our team was able to spend several hours with the girls the day we visited the training center, just long enough to fall in love with them. It made us want to minister to them in as many ways as we can, so we're developing a partnership with the center. We hope to provide both spiritual and financial support to the center and to the girls. We returned in September 2011, to share with them that they can find true identity and value in the eyes of Jesus Christ. We also hope to provide employment for the girls through Kairos Jewelry. And we plan to find ways to continue in relationship with them throughout their time at the center.

The Frankadua Girls' Vocational Training Center is a beautiful example of the rescue mission God calls His children to participate in. And it has captured my heart. The *girls* have captured my heart. If anyone needs to know Hagar's God, "the God who sees me," it is the trokosi—stolen, defiled, and discarded as garbage by the world. God, the great Rescuer, will move heaven and earth to position His rescue agents where they can reach these ones who are precious in His sight.

I want to be one of those agents.

"Taste and see that the Lord is good.

Oh, the joys of those who take refuge in him!...
The Lord is close to the broken-hearted;
He rescues those who are crushed in spirit."

Psalm 34:8, 18

2/11/2011

Lord Jesus, give Lauren a huge hug and kiss for me. Tell her I love her and miss her like crazy, and I'm living joyfully on mission for Your Kingdom, looking forward to the day we'll be together again forever.

Our team surrounded by the girls on our April, 2011 visit to the Frankadua Girls Vocational Training Center.

Several girls with me at our one day conference in
September 2011.

Chapter 12—Precious Gifts

From the very day of Lauren's accident, God began to pour out on us what I've come to call "gifts"—of His presence, of His words, and of Lauren. I told the story of the young man who was in the crowd gathered at our church that Monday evening, February 11, 2008. He gave us words that he, and we, believe were from God to us: "Good job. I love you." This message told our hearts: "Lauren has made it home, and I am pleased with her." What a precious gift! Over the next several months, we continued to receive gifts like this that assured us God was with us and Lauren was with Him. I want to share a few with you now.

Community Garden Coming Soon

We got home from the church late on the night of the accident. Some of our family from out of town were already there with us, and for awhile, we just sat together in a daze. When we finally got up to go to bed, Scott made the rounds to lock up. At the front door, he looked out onto the porch and saw a package. It had been delivered earlier in the day, and when Scott saw it, he immediately sensed God saying it was from Him. "Thank You, Lord," he whispered.

Scott brought the box in and opened it. Inside was a Precious Moments figurine entitled "Community Garden Coming Soon." It depicted a young girl on her knees planting seeds. For Scott, this was a clear message that God was going to bring a great harvest from the seeds of Lauren's life, a harvest we would all soon celebrate together in God's coming Kingdom.

What made this seem to be a gift from God, along with the strong impression Scott had that night, was the way it ended up on our porch on February 11th that year. I receive a Precious Moments membership figurine every year from Scott's parents for my birthday. For many years, it came on or near my actual birthday, April 16th. But several years ago the company started sending the figurines all at the same time to those with birthdays from January through June. I never know when I will get mine each year. In 2011, it came in mid-March. But in 2008, it came on February 11th.

Rebecca's Dream

At the time of the accident, I was leading a discipleship study in my home. This precious group included two women who have daughters close to Lauren. The women are dear friends of mine, so we continued to meet after the accident. They're part of the body of Christ who held me together during those first traumatic weeks.

Not long after the accident, one of these friends, Rebecca, shared a dream she had in which she was talking to Lauren. "I can't be talking to you," she told Lauren. "You're dead." Lauren answered, "No I'm not." "Yes you are." "No. I'm not." They repeated this several times, Lauren becoming more adamant each time before the dream ended.

When Rebecca told me the dream, I realized God had allowed Lauren to tell us she wasn't dead at all, but very much alive. This is what the Holy Spirit had been saying to me through scriptures like the one from my sister the first week: *"I tell you the truth, those who listen to my message and believe in God who sent me have eternal life. They will never be condemned for their sins, but **they have already passed from death into life**"* (John 5:24). And like the verse on a small framed print of an empty tomb that came to the house the day of Lauren's memorial service: *"I am the resurrection and the life. Anyone who believes in me **will live, even after dying**. Everyone who lives in me and believes in me **will never ever die**"* (John 11:25).

Lauren is alive, and she got to tell us that herself.

A Hug

About two months after the accident, I was washing my face to get ready for bed. Leaning over the sink and thinking about nothing in particular, I suddenly felt arms around my waist and someone lying across my back. A picture of Lauren burst into my mind with incredible force. It was so real that I immediately turned to embrace her, water dripping from my face. Of course she wasn't physically there, but I could feel her presence as strongly as though she was. It was a precious moment, one in which I believe God allowed Lauren to reach me with her love.

"Finally Home"

In the months following Lauren's home-going, there were several amazing songs on the radio. They spoke of the wonderful future God's children have with Christ and about our reunion with each other. Many times, more than I can write here, God used a song to speak hope to my hurting heart at just the right moment. One of them was called "Finally Home," by MercyMe. It's about a man who arrives in heaven, is joyfully reunited with his father, and meets Jesus face to face. It ministered incredibly to my broken heart every time I heard it. One day as I worked around the house, I asked God for the umpteenth time to please let me come Home. I was so tired of hurting and being crushed by the weight of the thought of being away from Lauren for years to come. Suddenly I heard, almost audibly, the words "Turn on the radio so you can hear 'Finally Home.'" They seemed like an answer to my question, and they came out of nowhere. They were spoken with such authority that I knew they weren't my own thoughts. So I turned on the radio.

After two songs, "Finally Home" played. I cried as it did, and part way through I heard the same voice as before say "It will be worth it all when you are finally home." Immediately, a verse came to my mind that God gave me a few weeks before through my precious friend, Courtney. *"Those who have been ransomed by the Lord will return to Jerusalem, singing songs of everlasting joy. Sorrow and mourning will disappear, and they will be overcome with joy and gladness"* (Isaiah 51:11). It had become the picture in my mind of my reunion with Lauren.

I rushed to my Bible to make a note beside that verse of the promise God had just given me. But when I opened to Isaiah 51, I saw something written beside verse 11: "When I see Lauren again, Finally Home." It was already there! I'm weeping while I write this, as I did that day, knowing that God twice gave me an unmistakable promise: every minute of my sorrow and mourning will truly be worth it when I am overcome with joy and gladness on that glorious day when I am "Finally Home."

A Note from Lauren

One summer night in 2008, I was traveling home from Tahlequah, about an hour from home. I was missing Lauren extra badly, and in a moment of weakness I asked God if I could please hear from her. I immediately felt it was a mistake to ask this, because I knew God forbids communication with those who have died. So I promptly put the idea out of my mind.

Earlier in the day, my mom had called and asked me to look for a book she thought I might have. When I got home that night, I went to the bookshelf where I kept it. I couldn't find it. So after double- and triple-checking, I went looking in the other bookcases around the house. When I got to the last one, the one in my bedroom, I saw a Mother's Day card Jonathan made me a couple of years before. Distracted from my search, I sat down to read through the little booklet. Stuck between two of the pages was a folded sheet of paper. I opened it and through tears, I recognized Lauren's handwriting. It was a Mother's Day note to me from a couple of years before. I didn't remember it, so the words seemed new:

> Mommy,
>
> Happy Mother's day! Wow Mom how do I even start? You're just so wonderful! Whatever I do, good or bad you always forgive me and then forget it! You're the best person (mom) that I could ever ask for! I look up to you in so many ways! I love how you're such a strong Christian ✞ thanks for just always being there for me!
>
> You're more than a mom to me you're my BFF!

What a precious and tender gift Jesus gave me from my daughter that night! I made a desperate plea from a mother's broken heart in a moment of weakness, and He honored it in perfect holiness.

A few weeks later, Mom brought me another copy of the book I couldn't find that night. I went to put the new copy in the bookshelf, and what did I find in plain sight? The first copy, the one that was nowhere to be found the night I had to go looking for it and found Lauren's note instead.

A Dream in Ghana

Our first night in Ghana on the youth mission trip, I had a dream. Here's my journal entry describing it:

6/20/2010

I dreamed about Lauren last night for the first time in many months. In the dream, Lauren was with me and she would say, "I want to be with you Mommy." I kept her close by me, so she went wherever I went. She kept saying "I just want to be with you. I miss you." Later in the dream, I could see her in the distance dancing with some children.

I think God is letting me know that Lauren knows we're here and that she's here with us. Thank you Jesus, for letting me be with her last night, and for letting her be part of this week. Tell her how much I love and miss her, and how I can't wait to celebrate what God is doing here in Ghana, as well as her part in it.

A Word about "Gifts"

I'm very thankful for the many gifts God gave us during our worst days of grief. They seem to be a common factor in the grief stories of believers. I've read some and I've heard others personally. Our God is a God of great mercy toward His children.

But none of the gifts we received are what our faith is based on, nor should they be. Our faith from start to finish is in the One True God revealed in the person of Jesus Christ and in His Word. The gifts, what Jesus called "signs," merely point us to the truth, and they seem to be used when the truth is new or hard to see. Jesus used them in His earthly ministry to illustrate the new covenant of grace and forgiveness, and the reality of God's coming Kingdom.

He warned the people, however, against depending upon signs for belief.

8/19/2009

"'Only an evil, faithless generation would ask for a miraculous sign, but the only sign I will give them is the sign of the prophet Jonah.' Then Jesus left them and went away."

Matthew 16:4

"Testing [Jesus] to see if he was from God, they demanded, 'Give us a miraculous sign from heaven to prove yourself.'

"When he heard this, he sighed deeply and said, 'Why do you people keep demanding a miraculous sign? I assure you, I will not give this generation any such sign.'"

Mark 8:12

God has given me many signs and messages of His faithfulness, love, and promises. I'm so thankful for His abundant goodness to me in this way. But I don't want to be dependent upon signs, or worse, become addicted to them. I don't want to become someone who continually says, "You must show us a miraculous sign if you want us to believe in you. What will you do for us?" (John 6:30)

I don't want to need more and more signs to keep believing God. I want my faith in Him to continue growing strong so that I can stand firmly

> *on His Word. I want roots that go deep into the*
> *foundation of the Lord Jesus Christ.*

In John 6, Jesus says over and over, "*I will raise them at the last day,*" and "*anyone who believes in me will live forever.*" His death and resurrection became the bedrock, the proof, of these claims. Nothing else is needed. They're the foundation—the only foundation—upon which to build a life of faith in Christ. The gifts or signs God gives His children are the loving touches of a tender-hearted Shepherd as He carries them through the valleys of this life. To build upon them as though they are the foundation leads only to disaster. God will not give us signs forever because He rightly wants our faith to be where it belongs: in His Son. Jesus proved for all time the extravagant love of God upon the cross. When the signs end, if we have built, or rebuilt, our faith upon them instead of on Christ, that "faith" will come crashing down.

> *Jesus, I want only to say, "Lord, to whom would*
> *I go? You alone have the words that give eternal*
> *life. I believe them and I know You are the Holy*
> *One of God." (See John 6:68-69.)*

Chapter 13—Grieving with Others

I've told my story of grief and healing under the loving care of my Counselor, the Holy Spirit of Jesus Christ. It was an intensely personal journey. But I didn't take it alone, even humanly speaking. In the next few paragraphs I want to share some of the opportunities God gave me to walk beside others who love Lauren and grieved her home-going deeply. I was able to minister to them by sharing things the Holy Spirit taught me, and they in turn ministered to me.

Let me speak a moment to fellow grievers. Though your own grief journey is undoubtedly a difficult one, please don't let Satan deceive you into "protecting" yourself by shutting off from others who are hurting. You may feel like you have nothing to give, and it may seem unfair that they would want something from you. It may feel like you have earned the right to crawl off and "lick your wounds," too broken to help anyone else. But that will only rob you of God's healing in your own life and isolate you from those who mourn the loss as deeply as you do. Reaching out will not only help heal them, but you as well.

Our Family

By 4:00 pm on February 11th, just minutes after we received the news of Lauren's departure from this world, we knew our family was at great risk. Statistics are dismal for the survival of families after the loss of a child. We didn't want to become one of those numbers, so we instinctively reached for each other—physically, relationally and spiritually. From the beginning, Scott and I talked and cried openly with each other. We explored all the painful feelings we had, from the many ways we blamed ourselves to all our dreams for Lauren that we would now have to let go of. We prayed together when we were too weak to endure the pain any longer.

We also talked about all that God was teaching us. Scott grabbed hold of God's goodness in bad times from the very start, while I, as should be clear by now, wrestled with it horribly. His tenacious refusal to see anything but God's goodness and purpose in our tragedy did much to drive me to God's Word for assurance to do the same.

We did all this right in front of our boys, never hiding our questions, pain, feelings of failure, or the hope we clung to like a lifeline. We talked often of Lauren's new life in heaven and what we were learning about it.

Jordan, nineteen at the time and our oldest, has always been able to express himself easily, so I could monitor his progress through grief fairly well. But Jonathan, only twelve, was never one to talk about his deeper feelings and struggles. Because he was in the accident and had actually seen Lauren trapped under the car, he had devastating memories to deal with. And we couldn't help him unless he shared them with us.

Except for Jonathan's immediate brief account of jumbled images from the accident on the first night, we couldn't get him to talk about it at all. We eventually learned that he felt it was his burden to carry the memories alone, because he didn't want to hurt us any more than we already were. But early on, when we got the police report and heard the medical examiner's findings, we pressed him for clarification and more details, to no avail.

At one point, God allowed us to learn of something Jonathan told friends that he was struggling with. He blamed himself for the fact that Lauren wasn't buckled. He saw that she didn't buckle when she got back into the car at Scott's office, but he didn't say anything to her about it. In his mind, that made it his fault she was thrown from the car, while he, buckled in, remained safe. Learning this gave us the opportunity to share with him our own feelings of guilt and self-blame. We assured him that no one blamed him, and we helped him at least begin to consider that he really wasn't at fault.

Over the next year, Scott and I watched Jonathan carefully. His grades never suffered, unlike those of many of Lauren's friends. He behaved respectfully and lovingly at home, and his relationships with friends, leaders at church and teachers at school were all good. We caught glimpses of his feelings when he posted on Lauren's Facebook wall, and when he wrote out his testimony on a Super Summer Leadership Camp application. He was hurting, but it appeared that he had made the critical choice to lean heavily on the Lord instead of turn away from Him. Yet he still refused to talk about either the accident or his grief.

One day, I shared my concerns about Jonathan with my friend Chris, a marriage and family therapist. Chris asked me about the various aspects of Jonathan's life—school, family, friends, church. When I told him all seemed well—

really well, in fact—he made a very insightful observation. Teenagers, he said, don't have the ability to hold something that big inside. If they don't talk about it or process it in some way, it will come out in destructive ways. Since Jonathan seemed to be functioning well in every area, Chris thought this indicated that he must be working through his grief. He then asked me how Scott and I dealt with our grief. When I told him we talked about everything right in front of and with the boys, he felt pretty certain that Jonathan was processing his grief *through us.*

I sensed this was true, but I continued to watch him. And time showed this to be the case for Jonathan. One day, about two years after the accident, I came across a couple of paragraphs in a grief book. In them, the author encouraged people not to judge others by the way they grieved. He described someone whose makeup predisposed him to process things on the inside, someone who didn't need to outwardly work through trouble or grief.

When Jonathan got home from school that afternoon, I handed him the book and asked him to read the paragraphs. He looked up when he finished and simply said, "I think that's me." I had my answer. And how I thanked God that Scott and I, and even Jordan, had been able to openly express every aspect of our grief. It gave Jonathan the guidance he needed to maneuver successfully through the minefield of grief in his own way.

One of the ways I intentionally shared with Jonathan the truths I was learning about heaven was to read with him the book *Heaven for Kids*, by Randy Alcorn. It's a condensed and less-detailed version of his book called *Heaven*, which was crucial to my survival. Reading *Heaven for Kids* every morning to Jonathan was a wonderful way to talk about

Lauren's new home. It helped him internalize his own hope in God's promise that his sister is alive and he'll see her again one day.

On the third anniversary of Lauren's home-going, I asked Jonathan how he was doing. His answer: "Better than last year." And in June, he told me that looking at Lauren's pictures on Facebook just used to make him sad. But when he looks at them now it makes him smile, because he knows they'll be together again one day. I know it too.

Remember how Jonathan made a "decision" to invite Jesus to be his Savior as a child, but that I knew it didn't guarantee his heart would trust Him in true relationship? Sharing his change of heart when he looked at Lauren's pictures was part of sharing his spiritual journey with me. The Holy Spirit opened Jonathan's heart that June to God's love for Him in Jesus Christ. For the first time, Jonathan truly surrendered his heart in love and trust to Christ. Now, my formerly non-communicative youngest son talks regularly with me about what God is teaching him and doing in his life. I am seeing the fruit of salvation in him that I knew would come when he gave Jesus his life. I am so grateful to God for His continuing faithfulness to our family.

Lauren's Friends

Lauren's friends began to arrive at the church on February 11th shortly after we did. As each one came and I looked at their precious crumpled faces and pain-filled eyes, I experienced something I never expected—deep compassion and love. I felt connected to them by our shared love for Lauren and the darkness we'd been plunged into.

The next day, Kathryn, Lauren's best friend literally from birth, was over at the house. We sat together on the couch and talked about Sunday, the day before the accident—the last day she and Lauren spent together. To my amazement, Kathryn told me they talked about their plans for the rest of their lives together. Like most teenage girls, these plans included dreams about living somewhere fun (in their case, Colorado), getting married, and raising a family, all as best friends forever. But then the plans took a surprising turn. Kathryn said Lauren began to talk about her funeral and what she wanted it to be like. She wanted Jordan to sing, and she wanted it to be a party, because she was not afraid to die. She knew she would be with Jesus. What a blessing for us to know and do the things Lauren wanted, and for Kathryn to have the privilege of contributing to the day that would honor her best friend.

Over the next few weeks, many of Lauren's friends came to our house. They recounted stories about my joy-filled, sometimes outrageous daughter. They were very open about her impact on their lives, most of which was very positive. Even previously "off-limits to parents" information, like her latest crush on a boy at school, was now freely shared with me. Talking about her seemed to help us all keep her close in those first excruciating days of separation. As a result of these precious times, I developed sweet relationships with three of Lauren's closest friends.

Before I share how God used me in each of their lives (and them in mine), let me talk briefly about the whole group of Lauren's church friends. She was an integral part of the youth group, one of the "spark plugs" that led others by example to find joy in Christ and share it with others. When she went home to Jesus, it drew the students together to carry on the desires of her heart. But the grief they experienced was real and deep, and they reached out to our family for help.

On Lauren's seventeenth birthday, just one month after the accident, all of her friends gathered at our house, maybe because to be in her house and close to us was to be close to her. For us it was the same. Having our house filled with kids and adults who love our precious daughter was a balm to our hearts. Scott and I both took the opportunity to share our hope in Christ with those kids, many of whom didn't have the family support to give them that hope.

At one point, I took the junior girls from church—Lauren's D-group—to my room so I could share with them a beautiful passage from Randy Alcorn's book *Heaven:*

> "Meanwhile, we on this dying Earth can relax and rejoice for our loved ones who are in the presence of Christ. As the apostle Paul tells us, though we naturally grieve at losing loved ones, we are 'not to grieve like the rest of men, who have no hope' (I Thessalonians 4:13). Our parting is not the end of our relationship, only an interruption. We have not 'lost' them, because we know where they are. They are experiencing the joy of Christ's presence in a place so wonderful that Christ called it Paradise. And one day, we're told, in a magnificent reunion, they and we 'will be with the Lord forever. Therefore, encourage each other with these words' (I Thessalonians 4:17-18)."[24]

Some of the girls have since told me they were able to hold on, through the worst of their grief, to God's promises

---

24 Alcorn, 73.

that they would see Lauren again because we were holding so firmly to them.

Three of Lauren's closest friends, Kathryn, Kacey, and Kristina, struggled fiercely with Lauren's loss in their lives. I'm thankful that God paved the way, in our first weeks of grief, for me to be able to walk through at least some of it with them. I like to believe I was able to help them sort through their pain and heartache, for they certainly ministered to me by loving my daughter. Each one of them has a unique history and relationship with Lauren, so their struggles were different, as were our ways of encouraging each other. Over the next three years, I got to spend time with them one on one. To this day, our relationships are a treasure to me.

I gave to each of the girls a three-by-five ringed card set filled with many of the scriptures God gave me about His presence, promises and peace. (These are listed under the Resources section at the end of the book.) I wanted them to know the greatest wellspring of help they could ever have to guide them through hard times. In return, the girls each told me precious stories and gave me love-filled pictures of them with Lauren. Kacey shared scriptures and songs with me that had ministered to her. Kathryn gave me a quilt she made from Lauren's t-shirts. She has also made a scripture card set for a friend going through a tough time. And Kristina nicknamed me "Momma Crawley." Several of Lauren's friends still call me that, and I love it.

Though we were initially drawn to each other by our mutual love for Lauren and the grief we were all struggling through, I have come to love them as the unique and special young women they are. I can never replace Lauren, nor do I need or want to, because I'll be with her again forever. But I feel as though I've gained three daughters in Christ. And I know Lauren is pleased that we've been there for each other in her absence.

Kacey, Lauren, Kristina, and Kathryn

Best friends

Afterword

What a gift from God it's been to look back over my journey with Him through grief and healing. As I wrote the story of my three years of grief counseling with the Holy Spirit, I saw just how far He brought me under His expert care. Going back to my journals—the record of His counsel and my healing—I learned even more. What a treasure God's Word is! How blessed we are to have it. It's a priceless resource given to us at enormous cost. Don't let the world fool you into believing it has no relevance today. It's to our peril that we ignore this most wonderful gift.

Since Lauren's accident, I have, unfortunately, had friends start their own grief journeys. Until I wrote this book, I didn't have a clear idea of how to help them. I just listened and shared bits and pieces of what God was teaching me when they seemed relevant. Today I still know that each person's needs and outlook are unique and should be treated as such. But now I always urge them to seek God in His Word, to let the Holy Spirit counsel them through their grief. This is because I understand so much better how unlimited, though often untapped, are the resources of the

Holy Spirit working through God's Word. He meets each of us where we are and helps us through even our darkest valleys. My journals are full of scripture, much more than what I shared here. So I always point fellow strugglers to the Bible and to Jesus.

No matter what any of us face in this life, Jesus has walked through it before us. No matter how deep our sorrow and pain, His grace and truth go deeper. No matter how long the road, He never leaves us. And so my one unchanging message, regardless of the struggle, sorrow, or pain someone faces, is "Go to God's Word, call on the name of Jesus, and let His Spirit counsel you with His infinite wisdom and hope." I tell them how the Holy Spirit called me to sit with Him daily, and how I did, sometimes for hours. And I say "No matter what it takes, make that time for Him." There is no greater wisdom, no sweeter love, no higher hope. Truly, *"anyone who trusts in him will never be disappointed"* (1 Peter 2:6). What a gift!

> *"And we have received God's Spirit (not the world's spirit), so we can know the wonderful things God has freely given us."*

> 1 Corinthians 2:12

Resources

Scriptures of God's Presence, Peace, Promise, and Purpose

Presence

Since Christ lives within you, even though your body will die because of sin, your spirit is alive because you have been made right with God. The Spirit of God, who raised Jesus from the dead, lives in you. And just as He raised Christ from the dead, He will give life to your mortal body by this same Spirit living within you. Romans 8:10-11

Can anything separate me from Christ's love? Does it mean He no longer loves me if I have trouble or calamity, or are persecuted, or are hungry or cold or in danger or threatened with death?...No, despite all these things, overwhelming victory is ours through Christ who loves me. And I am convinced that nothing can ever separate me from His love. Death can't, and life can't. The angels can't and the demons can't. My fears for today, my worries about tomorrow, and even the powers of hell can't keep God's love away. Whether we are high above the sky or in the deepest ocean, nothing in all creation will ever be able to separate me from the love of God that is revealed in Christ Jesus my Lord. Romans 8:35, 37-39

Thank God for His Son—a gift too wonderful for words!
2 Corinthians 9:15

Long ago, even before He made the world, God loved us and chose us in Christ to be holy and without fault in His eyes. His unchanging plan has always been to adopt us into His own family by bringing us to Himself through Jesus Christ. And this gave him great pleasure. Ephesians 1:4-5

Yet I still belong to you;
you are holding my right hand.
You will keep on guiding me with your counsel,
leading me to a glorious destiny.
Whom have I in heaven but you?
I desire you more than anything on earth.
My health may fail, and my spirit may grow weak,
but God remains the strength of my heart;
He is mine forever. Psalm 73:23-26

You will show me the way of life,
granting me the joy of your presence,
and the pleasures of living with you forever. Psalm 16:11

And God has given us His Spirit as proof that we live in Him and He in us. Furthermore, we have seen with our own eyes and now testify that the Father sent his Son to be the Savior of the world. All who proclaim that Jesus is the Son of God have God living in them, and they live in God. We know how much God loves us and we have put our trust in Him. 1 John 4:13-16

All praise to the God and Father of our Lord Jesus Christ. He is the source of every mercy and the God who comforts us. 2 Corinthians 1:3

I know the Lord is always with me.
I will not be shaken, for he is right beside me. Psalm 16:8

Don't be afraid, for I am with you. Do not be dismayed,
for I am your God. I will strengthen you. I will help you. I will
uphold you with my victorious right hand. Isaiah 41:10

I will never fail you.
I will never forsake you. Hebrews 13:5

Peace

We demolish arguments and every pretension that sets itself
up against the knowledge of God, and we take captive every
thought to make it obedient to Christ. 2 Corinthians 10:5

You will keep in perfect peace all who trust in you,
Whose thoughts are fixed on you! Isaiah 26:3

I am leaving you with a gift—peace of mind and heart.
And the peace I give isn't like the peace the world gives. So don't
be troubled or afraid. —Jesus, John 14:27

I have told you all this so that you may have peace in me.
Here on earth you will have many trials and sorrows. But take
heart, because I have overcome the world. —Jesus, John 16:33

Don't worry about anything; instead, pray about everything.
Tell God what you need, and thank him for all he has done. If
you do this, you will experience God's peace, which is far more
wonderful than the human mind can understand. His peace
will guard your hearts and minds as you live in Christ Jesus.
Philippians 4:6-7

Let us fix our eyes on Jesus, the author and perfecter of our faith, who for the joy set before him endured the cross, scorning its shame and sat down at the right hand of the throne of God. Consider him who endured such opposition from sinful men, so that you will not grow weary and lose heart. Hebrews 12:2-3 (NIV)

If your sinful nature controls your mind, there is death. But if the Holy Spirit controls your mind, there is life and peace. Romans 8:6

Promise

For God so loved the world that he gave his only Son, so that everyone who believes in Him will not perish but have eternal life. John 3:16

But God showed his great love for us by sending Christ to die for us while we were still sinners. Romans 5:8

God showed us how much He loved us by sending His only Son into the world so that we might have eternal life through him. 1 John 4:9

He (God) canceled the record that contained the charges against us. He took it and destroyed it by nailing it to Christ's cross. In this way, God disarmed the evil rulers and authorities. He shamed them publicly by his victory over them on the cross of Christ. Colossians 2:14-15

It has happened at last—the salvation and power and kingdom of our God, and the authority of his Christ! For the Accuser has been thrown down to earth—the one who accused our brothers and sisters before our God day and night. And they have defeated him because of the blood of the Lamb and because of their testimony. And they were not afraid to die. Revelation 12:10-11

For our present troubles are quite small and won't last very long. Yet they produce for us an immeasurably great glory that will last forever! So we don't look at the troubles we can see right now; rather we look forward to what we have not yet seen. For the troubles we see will soon be over, but the joys to come will last forever. 2 Corinthians 4:17-18

But we are citizens of heaven where the Lord Jesus Christ lives. And we are eagerly waiting for him to return as our Savior. He will take these weak mortal bodies of ours and change them into glorious bodies like his own, using the same mighty power that he will use to conquer everything, everywhere. Philippians 3:20-21

For we know that when this earthly tent we live in is taken down—when we die and leave these bodies—we will have a home in heaven, an eternal body make for us by God himself and not by human hands. We grow weary in our present bodies, and we long for the day when we will put on our heavenly bodies like new clothing. For we will not be spirits without bodies, but we will put on new heavenly bodies. Our dying bodies make us groan and sigh but it's not that we want to die and have no bodies at all. We want to slip into our new bodies so that these dying bodies will be swallowed up by everlasting life. God himself has prepared us for this, and as a guarantee he has given us his Holy Spirit. So we are always confident, even though we know that as long as we live in these bodies we are not at home with the Lord. That is why we live by believing and not by seeing. Yes, we are fully confident, and we would rather be away from these bodies, for then we will be at home with the Lord. 2 Corinthians 5:1-8

The fact is that Christ has been raised from the dead. He has become the first of a great harvest of those who will be raised to life again. 1 Corinthians 15:20

But let me tell you a wonderful secret God has revealed to us. Not all of us will die, but we will all be transformed. It will happen in a moment, in the blinking of an eye, when the last trumpet is blown. For when the trumpet sounds, the Christians who have died will be raised with transformed bodies. And then we who are living will be transformed so that we will never die. 1 Corinthians 15:51-52

And now, brothers and sisters, I want you to know what will happen to the Christians who have died so you will not be full of sorrow like people who have no hope. For since we believe that Jesus died and was raised to life again, we also believe that when Jesus comes, God will bring back with Jesus all the Christians who have died. I can tell you this directly from the Lord: We who are still living when the Lord returns will not rise to meet him ahead of those who are in their graves. For the Lord himself will come down from heaven with a commanding shout, with the call of the archangel, and with the trumpet call of God. First, all the Christians who have died will rise from their graves. Then, together with them, we who are still alive and remain on the earth will be caught up in the clouds to meet the Lord in the air and remain with him forever. 1 Thessalonians 4:13-17

> *Yet we have this assurance:*
> *Those who belong to God will live;*
> *their bodies will rise again!*
> *Those who sleep in the earth*
> *will rise up and sing for joy!*
> *For God's light of life will fall like dew*
> *on his people in the place of the dead!* Isaiah 26:19

In Jerusalem, the Lord Almighty will spread a wonderful feast for everyone around the world. It will be a delicious feast of good food, with clear, well-aged wine and choice beef. In that day he will remove the cloud of gloom, the shadow of death that hangs over the earth. He will swallow up death forever! The Sovereign Lord will wipe away all tears. He will remove forever all insults and mockery against his land and people. The Lord has spoken. In that day the people will proclaim, "This is our God. We trusted in him, and he saved us. This is the Lord, in whom we trusted. Let us rejoice in the salvation he brings! Isaiah 25:6-9

Those who have been ransomed by the Lord will return to Jerusalem, singing songs of everlasting joy. Sorrow and mourning will disappear, and they will be overcome with joy and gladness. Isaiah 51:11

But as for me, I know that my Redeemer lives, and that he will stand on the earth at last. And after my body has decayed, yet in my body I will see God! I will see him for myself. Yes, I will see him with my own eyes. I am overwhelmed at the thought! Job 19:25-27

At that time every one of your people whose name is written in the book will be rescued. Many of those whose bodies lie dead and buried will rise up, some to everlasting life and some to shame and everlasting contempt...As for you, go your way until the end. You will rest, and then at the end of the days, you will rise again to receive the inheritance set aside for you. Daniel 12:1b-2, 13

I heard a loud shout from the throne, saying, "Look, the home of God is now among his people! He will live with them, and they will be his people. God himself will be with them. He will remove all their sorrows, and there will be no more death or sorrow or crying or pain. For the old world and its evils are gone forever." And the one sitting on the throne said, "Look, I am making all things new!" And he said to me, "Write this down, for what I tell you is trustworthy and true." Revelation 21:3-5

See, I am coming soon, and my reward is with me, to repay all according to their deeds. I am the Alpha and the Omega, the First and the Last, the beginning and the end. –King Jesus, Revelation 22:12-13

Then everyone will see the Son of Man arrive on the clouds with great power and glory. And he will send forth his angels to gather together his chosen ones from all over the world—from the farthest ends of the earth and heaven. –Jesus, Mark 13:26-27

Don't be so surprised! Indeed, the time is coming when all of the dead in their graves will hear the voice of God's Son, and they will rise again. –Jesus, John 5:28-29a

Purpose

May the Lord bring you into an ever deeper understanding of the love of God and the endurance that comes from Christ. 2 Thessalonians 3:5

He comforts us in all our troubles so that we can comfort others. When others are troubled, we will be able to give them the same comfort God has given us. You can be sure that the more we suffer for Christ, the more God will shower us with his comfort through Christ. 2 Corinthians 1:4-5

For to me, living is for Christ, and dying is even better. Yet if I live, that means fruitful service for Christ. I really don't know which is better. I'm torn between two desires: Sometimes I want to live, and sometimes I long to go and be with Christ. That would be far better for me, but it is better for you that I live. Philippians 1:21-24

But this precious treasure—this light and power that now shine within us—is held in perishable containers, that is, in our weak bodies. So everyone can see that our glorious power is from God and is not our own…Through suffering, these bodies of ours constantly share in the death of Jesus so that the life of Jesus may also be seen in our bodies. 2 Corinthians 4:7, 10

So our aim is to please him always, whether we are here in this body or away from this body. 2 Corinthians 5:6-9

For we are God's masterpiece. He has created us anew in Christ Jesus, so that we can do the good things he planned for us long ago. Ephesians 2:10

Recommended Grief Books

Heaven, by Randy Alcorn. Tyndale House Publishers, Inc., 2004.

Heaven for Kids, by Randy Alcorn. Tyndale House Publishers, Inc., 2006.

Confessions of a Grieving Christian, by Zig Ziglar. B & H Books, 2004.

When Loved Ones Are Called Home, by Herbert H. Wernecke. Baker Books, 1949.

Holding on to Hope, by Nancy Guthrie. Tyndale House Publishers, Inc., 2002.

Hope for the Brokenhearted, by Dr. John Luke Terveen. Victor/Cook Communications Ministries, 2006.

One on One with God
By Jerry and Marilyn Fine
www.1on1withgod.org

One on One with God, by Jerry and Marilyn Fine, is a 15-week discipleship course. It provides a path that leads to knowing Jesus personally, a lifestyle of walking daily in intimate fellowship with Him, and a tool for making disciples and producing disciple-makers. Though the course can be completed in 15 weeks, its purpose is to help participants develop and grow their ability to hear from God and respond to Him one on one for the rest of their lives here on earth. It also helps them live lives of daily surrender to the Holy Spirit for transformation to produce the fruit of Christ's character.

One on One with God provided me with the ability to pursue intimate relationship with Christ. This relationship was the context of my three years of grief counseling with the Holy Spirit in God's Word. *One on One* has also given me great spiritual understanding of the life Jesus came to give us. It's not a life built on rules or even disciplines, but on knowing Him and living daily out of the overflow of His Spirit as we surrender to Him.

Website information:

I pray that God has touched you through *Wonderful Counselor*, and that you will recommend it to others who might need it. I would love to hear how God is ministering to you through my story. Please visit the following website for more information about the author and related ministries: www.wonderfulcounselorthebook.com

CPSIA information can be obtained at www.ICGtesting.com
Printed in the USA
LVOW041224281111

256754LV00001B/7/P